Christian Wojek

Visual Scene Understanding from Mobile Platforms

Christian Wojek

Visual Scene Understanding from Mobile Platforms

A Monocular Approach

Südwestdeutscher Verlag für Hochschulschriften

Imprint
Any brand names and product names mentioned in this book are subject to trademark, brand or patent protection and are trademarks or registered trademarks of their respective holders. The use of brand names, product names, common names, trade names, product descriptions etc. even without a particular marking in this work is in no way to be construed to mean that such names may be regarded as unrestricted in respect of trademark and brand protection legislation and could thus be used by anyone.

Publisher:
Südwestdeutscher Verlag für Hochschulschriften
is a trademark of
Dodo Books Indian Ocean Ltd., member of the OmniScriptum S.R.L Publishing group
str. A.Russo 15, of. 61, Chisinau-2068, Republic of Moldova Europe
Printed at: see last page
ISBN: 978-3-8381-2049-2

Zugl. / Approved by: Darmstadt, Technische Universität, Dissertation, 2010

Copyright © Christian Wojek
Copyright © 2010 Dodo Books Indian Ocean Ltd., member of the OmniScriptum S.R.L Publishing group

ABSTRACT

Automatic visual scene understanding is one of the ultimate goals in computer vision and has been in the field's focus since its early beginning. Despite continuous effort over several years, applications such as autonomous driving and robotics are still unsolved and subject to active research. In recent years, improved probabilistic methods became a popular tool for current state-of-the-art computer vision algorithms. Additionally, high resolution digital imaging devices and increased computational power became available. By leveraging these methodical and technical advancements current methods obtain encouraging results in well defined environments for robust object class detection, tracking and pixel-wise semantic scene labeling and give rise to renewed hope for further progress in scene understanding for real environments.

This thesis improves state-of-the-art scene understanding with monocular cameras and aims for applications on mobile platforms such as service robots or driver assistance for automotive safety. It develops and improves approaches for object class detection and semantic scene labeling and integrates those into models for global scene reasoning which exploit context at different levels.

To enhance object class detection, we perform a thorough evaluation for people and pedestrian detection with the popular sliding window framework. In particular, we address pedestrian detection from a moving camera and provide new benchmark datasets for this task. As frequently used single-window metrics can fail to predict algorithm performance, we argue for application-driven image-based evaluation metrics, which allow a better system assessment. We propose and analyze features and their combination based on visual and motion cues. Detection performance is evaluated systematically for different feature-classifiers combinations which is crucial to yield best results. Our results indicate that cue combination with complementary features allow improved performance. Despite camera ego-motion, we obtain significantly better detection results for motion-enhanced pedestrian detectors.

Realistic onboard applications demand real-time processing with frame rates of 10 Hz and higher. In this thesis we propose to exploit parallelism in order to achieve the required runtime performance for sliding window object detection. In a case study we employ commodity graphics hardware for the popular histograms of oriented gradients (HOG) detection approach and achieve a significant speed-up compared to a baseline CPU implementation.

Furthermore, we propose an integrated dynamic conditional random field model for joint semantic scene labeling and object detection in highly dynamic scenes. Our model improves semantic context modeling and fuses low-level filter bank responses with more global object detections. Recognition performance is increased for object as well as scene classes. Integration over time needs to account for different dynamics of objects and scene classes but yields more robust results.

Finally, we propose a probabilistic 3D scene model that encompasses multi-class object detection, object tracking, scene labeling, and 3D geometric relations. This integrated 3D model is able to represent complex interactions like inter-object occlusion, physical exclusion between objects, and geometric context. Inference in this model allows to recover 3D scene context and perform 3D multi-object tracking from a mobile observer, for objects of multiple categories, using only monocular video as input. Our results indicate that our joint scene tracklet model for the evidence collected over multiple frames substantially improves performance.

All experiments throughout this thesis are performed on challenging real world data. We contribute several datasets that were recorded from moving cars in urban and sub-urban environments. Highly dynamic scenes are obtained while driving in normal traffic on rural roads. Our experiments support that joint models, which integrate semantic scene labeling, object detection and tracking, are well suited to improve the individual stand-alone tasks' performance.

ZUSAMMENFASSUNG

Automatisiertes visuelles Szenenverstehen gehört zu den letztendlichen Zielen des maschinellen Sehens und steht bereits seit dem Beginn der Forschungsaktivitäten im Zentrum des Interesses. Trotz mehrjähriger kontinuierlicher Bemühungen sind jedoch Anwendungen wie zum Beispiel autonomes Fahren und autonome Robotorsysteme noch immer ungelöst und Gegenstand aktiver Forschung. In den letzten Jahren entwickelten sich probabilistische Methoden zu einem beliebten Werkzeug für die Ansätze des maschinellen Sehens, die den derzeitigen Stand der Technik darstellen. Zusätzlich hat die Leistungsfähigkeit von Rechnern stark zugenommen und hochauflösende digitale Kamerasensoren wurden verfügbar. Gegenwärtige Ansätze nutzen diese methodischen und technischen Verbesserungen und erreichen in wohl definierten Umgebungen ermutigende Ergebnisse in den Bereichen robuste Objektklassenerkennung, Objektverfolgung und pixelweise semantische Szenensegmentierung. Diese geben Anlass zu erneuter Hoffnung auf Fortschritte im Gesamtszenenverständnis realistischer Umgebungen.

Diese Arbeit verbessert den Stand der Technik für monokulares Szenenverständnis und ist auf Anwendungsszenarien mit mobilen Plattformen wie zum Beispiel Servicerobotern oder Fahrerassistenzsystemen zur Erhöhung der automobilen Fahrsicherheit ausgerichtet. Sie entwickelt und verbessert Ansätze zur Objektklassendetektion und zur semantischen Szenensegmentierung und integriert diese in Modelle zum Gesamtszenenverständnis, die Kontext unterschiedlicher Art ausnutzen.

Zunächst führen wir zu einem besseren Verständnis der Objektklassenerkennung eine sorgfältige Leistungsanalyse unterschiedlicher Ansätze durch, die das Sliding-Window-Paradigma für die Erkennung von Menschen und Fußgängern verwenden. Insbesondere behandeln wir Fußgängererkennungsalgorithmen, die mit bewegten Kameras verwendet werden können und stellen für diese Aufgabe neue Vergleichsdatensätze zur freien Verfügung. Da häufig verwendete Einzelfenstermetriken bei der Bestimmung der Leistungsfähigkeit scheitern können, plädieren wir in dieser Arbeit für die Verwendung anwendungsorientierter Gesamtbildmetriken, die eine bessere Beurteilung erlauben. Darüber hinaus schlagen wir die Verwendung und Kombination von Aussehens- und Bewegungsmerkmalen vor und analysieren diese systematisch für verschiedene Klassifikator/Merkmalskombinationen. Dies erweist sich als wichtig, um die besten Ergebnisse zu erzielen. Unsere Ergebnisse zeigen, dass die Kombination komplementärer Merkmale zu einer verbesserten Erkennungsleistung führen kann. Trotz Kameraeigenbewegung erreichen wir unter Miteinbeziehung von Bewegungsmerkmalen bei der Detektion von Fußgängern signifikant bessere Ergebnisse.

Reale Anwendungen mit mobilen Plattformen benötigen häufig eine Echtzeitverarbeitungsgeschwindigkeit von 10 Bilder pro Sekunde und mehr. In dieser Arbeit schlagen wir vor, mögliche Parallelität von Verarbeitungsschritten auszunutzen, um diese Geschwindigkeit für das Sliding-Window-Verfahren zu erreichen. In einer Fallstudie verwenden wir Endbenutzergrafikhardware, um das verbreitete Histograms of oriented

Gradients (HOG) Erkennungsverfahren zu implementieren und erreichen damit eine signifikante Beschleunigung gegenüber einer CPU-basierten Referenzimplementierung. Des Weiteren schlagen wir ein integriertes dynamisches Conditional Random Field Modell vor, das die gleichzeitige Inferenz von semantischer Szenensegmentierung und die Erkennung von Objekten in hochdynamischen Szenen erlaubt. Unser Modell verbessert die Modellierung semantischen Kontextes und verbindet low-level Filterbankantworten mit Objekthypothesen. Dabei wird die Erkennungsleistung sowohl für Objekt- als auch für Hintergrundszenenklassen verbessert. Die zeit-dynamische Erweiterung des Modells beachtet die höchst unterschiedliche Bewegungsdynamik von Objekten und Hintergrundszene und kann dadurch noch robustere Ergebnisse erzielen.

Schließlich schlagen wir ein probabilistisches 3D Gesamtszenenmodell vor, das Mehrklassenobjektdetektion, Objektverfolgung, semantische Szenensegmentierung und die Modellierung von 3D Beziehungen vereint. Dieses integrierte 3D Modell ist in der Lage komplexe Wechselwirkungen wie Verdeckung unter Objekten, physikalischen Ausschluss von Objekten, sowie geometrischen Kontext zu modellieren. Dieses Modell erlaubt es, lediglich unter Verwendung einer monokularen Kamera, 3D Szenenkontext zu erschließen und mehrere Objekte unterschiedlicher Kategorien zu verfolgen. Unsere experimentellen Ergebnisse belegen, dass dieses integrierte Szenen-Tracklet-Modell, das Bildinformation mehrerer aufeinander folgender Eingabebilder benutzt, bedeutend bessere Ergebnisse erzielt.

Alle Experimente im Verlauf dieser Arbeit wurden mit anspruchsvollen, reellen Daten durchgeführt, die von fahrenden Autos in ländlichen und innerstädtischen Umgebungen aufgenommen wurden und zur freien Verfügung gestellt werden. Unsere Experimente belegen, dass die gleichzeitige Modellierung von semantischer Szenensegmentierung, Objekterkennung und -verfolgung gut dazu geeignet ist, die Leistungsfähigkeit der individuellen Komponenten weiter zu verbessern.

ACKNOWLEDGEMENTS

This thesis would not have been possible without the support and advice of many great people who contributed to this work in various ways. First, I would like to thank my supervisor Prof. Dr. Bernt Schiele for giving me the chance to learn about the fascinating world of computer vision in his lab. Throughout the course of this thesis (including long nights before submission deadlines) he supported my work with inspiring discussions and invaluable advice. I would also like to thank Prof. Dr. Stefan Roth and Prof. Dr. Konrad Schindler for providing me with additional guidance during my last year. I am also very grateful to Prof. Dr. Luc Van Gool for serving as external reviewer on my thesis committee.

Many thanks are due to Ursula Paeckel, who was very helpful in all administrative matters. Furthermore, I owe thanks to all members of the MIS, IU and ESS groups for inspiring discussions on research and non-research topics during retreats and coffee breaks: Anton Andriyenko, Eugen Berlin, Ulf Blanke, Marko Borazio, Victoria Carlsson, Gyuri Dorkó, Sandra Ebert, Tâm Huỳnh, Kristof Van Laerhoven, Diane Larlus, Nikodem Majer, Marcus Rohrbach, Paul Schnitzspan, Ulrich Steinhoff, Maja Stikic, Christoph Vogel, Stefan Walk, Zeeshan Zia and Andreas Zinnen. Especially, I would like to thank Edgar Seemann and Mario Fritz for being great tutors during the start of my thesis and my office mates Michael Stark and Micha Andriluka for many fruitful discussions. Further thanks go to Piotr Dollár at the California Institute of Technology for our good collaboration and many insightful phone conferences.

Also my students deserve some credit. In particular I would like to thank André Schulz for his constant efforts to speed up my algorithms. Further thanks go to my project colleagues Andree Hohm, Roman Mannale and Ken Schmitt for excellent collaboration on a real hardware (car) system.

Moreover, I would like to thank Continental Teves, Toyota Motor Europe and the EU project CoSy for providing my research not only with the necessary funding but also with challenging real world problems.

Finally, I would like to thank all my friends, in particular Bastian Rapp, and my family who supported me whenever necessary throughout my studies.

CONTENTS

1 Introduction   **1**
   1.1 Importance of automatic visual scene understanding 2
   1.2 Challenges for visual scene understanding 4
   1.3 Contributions of the thesis 10
   1.4 Outline of the document 11

2 Related Work   **15**
   2.1 Object detection 16
       2.1.1 Bottom-up object detection from local evidence 17
       2.1.2 Top-down object detection with global template models 19
       2.1.3 Relation to own work 27
   2.2 2D context and semantic scene labeling 28
       2.2.1 Object detection in 2D context 28
       2.2.2 Semantic scene labeling. 29
       2.2.3 Relation to own work 32
   2.3 Tracking 33
       2.3.1 Relation to own work 36
   2.4 3D scene understanding 37
       2.4.1 Relation to own work 40

3 Evaluation of Static Features for People Detection   **41**
   3.1 Introduction 42
   3.2 Features and classifiers 42
       3.2.1 Features 43
       3.2.2 Classifiers 45
   3.3 Dataset and methodology 45
   3.4 Evaluation criterion 46
   3.5 Experiments 47
       3.5.1 Single feature detection 47
       3.5.2 Multi-cue detection 48
       3.5.3 Failure analysis 52
   3.6 Conclusion 53

4 Multi-Cue Onboard Pedestrian Detection   **55**
   4.1 Introduction 55
   4.2 Features and classifiers 58
       4.2.1 Features 58
       4.2.2 Classifiers 59
   4.3 Learning and testing 60
       4.3.1 Improved learning procedure 60

		4.3.2 Testing	61
	4.4	New dataset	62
	4.5	Results	63
	4.6	Conclusion	69

5 Real-Time Object Detection 71
- 5.1 Introduction 71
- 5.2 Object class detection using HOG 72
- 5.3 Programming on the GPU 73
- 5.4 HOG on the GPU 74
- 5.5 Discussion on GPU implementations 77
- 5.6 Experiments 79
  - 5.6.1 Datasets 79
  - 5.6.2 Detection performance 81
  - 5.6.3 Runtime analysis 82
- 5.7 Conclusion 84

6 Dynamic CRFs for Scene Segmentation 85
- 6.1 Introduction 85
- 6.2 Conditional random field models 86
  - 6.2.1 Plain CRF: Single layer CRF model for scene-class labeling 87
  - 6.2.2 Object CRF: Two layer object CRF for joint object and scene labeling 87
  - 6.2.3 Dynamic CRF: Dynamic two layer CRF for object and scene class labeling 89
  - 6.2.4 Inference and parameter estimation 90
- 6.3 Experiments 91
  - 6.3.1 Features for scene labeling 91
  - 6.3.2 Results 93
- 6.4 Conclusion 98

7 Monocular 3D Scene Modeling and Inference 99
- 7.1 Introduction 99
- 7.2 Single-frame 3D scene model 101
  - 7.2.1 Inference framework 103
  - 7.2.2 Proposal moves 103
  - 7.2.3 Projective 3D to 2D marginalization 105
- 7.3 Multi-frame scene model and inference 105
  - 7.3.1 Multi-frame 3D scene tracklet model 105
  - 7.3.2 Long term data association with scene tracking 106
- 7.4 Datasets and implementation details 107
- 7.5 Experimental results 109
- 7.6 Conclusion 116

8	**Conclusion and Future Perspectives**	**117**
	8.1 Discussion of contributions	118
	8.2 Future perspectives	119

List of Figures   **125**

List of Tables   **129**

Bibliography   **131**

1 INTRODUCTION

Contents

1.1	Importance of automatic visual scene understanding	2
1.2	Challenges for visual scene understanding	4
1.3	Contributions of the thesis	10
1.4	Outline of the document	11

Although, first commercial automatic vision systems, like face detectors in digital cameras and lane departure warning systems in car safety applications, became recently available, the ultimate goal of computer vision to make computers "see" is far from being solved. Remarkable process has been made throughout the last decade, but still tremendous effort is required to develop automatic systems that understand scenes, even of low complexity, which can already be understood by infants.

For human perception Gibson's *Ecological Approach to Visual Perception* (1979) is one of the most accepted among psychologists. He established a *ground theory* that he describes as theory of the layout of surfaces: "By *layout*, I mean the relations of surfaces to the ground and to one another, their arrangement. The layout includes both places and objects, together with other features." According to Gibson, among all surfaces the ground plane has an outstanding role: "The ground outdoors or the floor indoors is the main surface of support. Animals have to be supported against gravity. If the layout of surfaces is to be substituted for space in the theory of perception, this *fundamental* surface should get first consideration." Gibson stresses the importance of *context* and states his view on human perception as simple as: "It's not what is inside the head that is important, it's what the head is inside of."

Similarly, researchers in computer vision have argued and modeled the fact that humans exploit context information in order to understand scenes. For instance, Torralba (2003) shows that context can even dominate human object recognition. In Figure 1.1 the object's pixel pattern in the front is identical in both images with the only difference of an orientation by 90 degrees and a shift of the pixels to the front in the right image. Guided by the context, humans perceive a car in the left image, but a pedestrian in the right image. Here, context is constituted by the street (i.e. the ground plane), the building in the background and the relative sizes to each other and their position with respect to the camera.

But not only can scene context facilitate object recognition; the reverse is also true. Hoiem *et al.* (2006), for instance, state: "Of course, just as scene and camera geometry can influence object detection, so can the detected objects alter the geometry estimation. For example, if we know the locations/scales of some of the objects in the image, we can use this to better estimate the camera viewpoint parameters."

(a) Object pattern perceived as car   (b) Object pattern perceived as pedestrian

Figure 1.1: An identical pattern perceived as car or pedestrian depending on the image context. Images are courtesy of Antonio Torralba (2003).

Consequently, improved context models as well as more robust detection of objects will allow to progress towards automatic understanding of scenes. Therefore, this thesis will not only investigate different contextual models for scene understanding but also object detection.

1.1 IMPORTANCE OF AUTOMATIC VISUAL SCENE UNDERSTANDING

While research on automatic scene understanding for general scenes has already emerged in the 1970s the complexity of real world environments impeded the success of the employed – often heuristic – methods. In particular, heavily cluttered backgrounds and objects with a high degree of articulation or a high intra-class variability such as pedestrians caused these methods' failure.

Recent advances in machine learning and probabilistic modeling allow to learn complex models and infer variables even when the number of parameters is large. These methods as well as success in the fields of object detection, segmentation and tracking have revived interest in scene understanding. This thesis is in this line of research and specifically focuses on the application scenario of scene understanding from mobile platforms such as cars or robots. These environments allow to exploit a high degree of prior knowledge, but are nonetheless important to several applications such as:

- Car safety, driver assistance and autonomous driving
- Service robots
- Space exploration robots
- Visual surveillance

In the field of driver assistance, robust detection of pedestrians is one of the most important tasks. The US Department of Transportation reports 4378 killed and 69.000

1.1 IMPORTANCE OF AUTOMATIC VISUAL SCENE UNDERSTANDING

injured pedestrians for the US in 2008[1]. Similarly, Destatis reports 653 killed and 32.770 injured pedestrians for Germany in 2008[2]. To reduce this number the EU commission started an initiative with the goal to halve the number of road fatalities by the year 2010. While other sensor modalities (e.g., RADAR) have successfully been used to detect vehicle traffic, they are less applicable to pedestrian detection. RADAR sensors often fail to detect pedestrians due to missing reflectance properties. For laser sensors the resolution is often too restricted for this task. Hence, detecting pedestrians in onboard camera images seems to be the most promising approach. Applications that can be built on a robust pedestrian detection system range from active control strategies such as evasion maneuvers and collision mitigation to passive strategies such as inflating an airbag at the car front or lifting the hood to avoid a run-over pedestrian to roll in front of the car. In particular, we are interested to detect pedestrians, who walk perpendicular to the own car's trajectory. These pedestrians are most likely to cross the street unexpectedly for the driver. In this thesis, we evaluate and advance the state-of-the-art for camera-based pedestrian detection with a focus on onboard scenarios. Even though motion is frequently considered an inappropriate cue for moving cameras, we show improved detection performance with motion-based features.

A further application scenario, which we investigated in the course of this thesis, is overtaking assistance. Our work has been embedded in the interdisciplinary research project PRORETA. The goal of this project was to recognize and assist overtaking maneuvers. This application demands robust detection of all traffic participants including the overtaken vehicle as well as all oncoming traffic. In particular, for the close range up to 100 m the information available in a video stream is a helpful cue. Positions of objects can be detected with a high lateral resolution. Therefore, this sensor information is complementary to other sensors like RADAR or laser scanners. But not only does the camera sensor allow the detection of objects in the close range; it also allows to determine the free space for evasion maneuvers by segmenting the image. This task can hardly be achieved at a high level of accuracy by any other sensor. For controlling highly dynamic systems, such as cars driving at a speed of around 100 km/h (60 miles/h), real-time requires extremely fast processing. Frame rates in the order of 15 Hz are desirable to achieve robust system performance. In a case study we show that state-of-the-art object detectors offer a high degree of parallelism that can be exploited to speed-up computation. We use a highly parallel graphics co-processor (GPU) to demonstrate real-time pedestrian and vehicle detection on VGA image resolution (640 × 480 pixel) with no loss in detection performance compared to a CPU implementation.

Another field of application to our research is robotics. Growing interest in automation and progress in several fields such as odometry, self localization and map building (Wang et al., 2007) make service robot applications more realistic. However, for the deployment in human populated environments robots will have to navigate safely and autonomously. Thus, they need to be able to detect humans and other objects robustly in order to avoid collisions. Moreover, human-computer interaction will be in the focus of this application domain. In order to initiate any kind of interaction humans need

---

[1]Figures reported in "National Highway Traffic Safety Administration Facts Sheet 2008".
[2]Figures reported in "Statistisches Jahrbuch 2009".

to be successfully detected and recognized beforehand. Further application domains are space missions involving robots on distant planets, e.g., on Mars. Due to extreme signal runtime ($\approx$ 20 minutes to Mars) robots will have to recognize the surrounding terrain and detect obstacles in order to navigate at least semi-autonomously. Search and rescue operations, e.g., after natural disasters are another task in robotics. Robots can, for instance, be used to search for victims in highly polluted and therefore dangerous sites. Any kind of ground based robotics application typically allow similar assumptions as the aforementioned car safety applications and consequently similar methods and models can be applied.

A further application domain is automated video surveillance. The terror acts of 2001 gave rise to an increased deployment of surveillance cameras. Within Europe the highest density of cameras can be found in the UK. Estimations assume several million cameras across the country. Undoubtedly, the vast amount of data can hardly be processed by humans and (semi-)automated methods need to be developed in order to take advantage of the collected information. Contrary to robotics and automotive applications, surveillance cameras are typically statically mounted. Hence, the problem of scene understanding is more constraint than from mobile platforms. Nonetheless, methods developed for moving cameras can be transferred to this domain and can be even further improved by exploiting the additional constraints. In the future, moving agents might appear for surveillance tasks as well in order to increase coverage. Challenging problems in this scenario are tracking of pedestrians, recognition of unusual events and aggression detection. All three tasks require the robust detection of humans. Typically, detection and tracking results can be drastically improved by a ground plane assumption. This requires a time-consuming camera calibration. In Chapter 7 of this thesis we will present a method, which is in principle transferable to this application domain, that performs joint inference on camera calibration, object positions and sizes.

1.2 CHALLENGES FOR VISUAL SCENE UNDERSTANDING

Understanding real world visual scenes in automotive and robotics environments is a challenging problem for multiple reasons. The following section discusses and illustrates challenges in more detail. We will start with the problems that are specific for the detection of objects, in particular of pedestrians. Later, we move on to complicating issues that arise in real-world environments and from mobile platforms.

Pedestrian articulation. Unlike cars, which have a rigid object layout, pedestrians are highly articulated. The human walking cycle, even though being constraint, allows for a number of different poses of legs and arms. The pedestrian shape, which is often considered to be the most discriminative feature, is constantly changing (cf. Figure 1.2). Thus, a pedestrian's representation with any kind of model either needs to be very flexible, for instance by having a notion of parts, or needs to be able to appropriately represent the multi-modal distribution of different poses.

Multiple viewpoints and intra-class variations. Moreover, pedestrians show a very

1.2 CHALLENGES FOR VISUAL SCENE UNDERSTANDING

Figure 1.2: Pedestrians with different articulations: standing, walking and running

high intra-class variation due to different clothing and physique. Clothing is highly individual and may have any kind of shape and color. It can range from voluminous winter coats and skirts to light summer dresses. Also people are small or tall, slim or corpulent. Both clothing and physique increase the shape variability considerably. Furthermore, pedestrians can walk on the ground with almost no constraints. Hence, they can appear from many viewpoints and spontaneously change their walking direction. Appearance from different viewpoints may vary greatly and is dependent on the walking cycle's current state. See Figure 1.3 for some challenging samples.

Figure 1.3: Pedestrians with varying appearance across different viewpoints, individual clothing style and physique

Object occlusion and carried accessories. A frequent challenge for pedestrian detection in urban environments is occlusion. In many dangerous situations people or even children suddenly appear between parking cars from the sidewalk and intend to cross the street. Consequently, the parking cars occlude the legs and alter the pedestrians shape drastically. Also pedestrians walking in a larger group of people occlude each other and therefore complicate the detection task. Similarly, accessories carried by pedestrians pose a problem. They often occlude part of the pedestrian or change the typical shape and proportion. Examples are backpacks, shopping bags or bicycles (cf. Figure 1.4).

Large scale range and small scale objects. In driver assistance systems the goal is to detect any kind of obstacle, including pedestrians, as early as possible to allow for a broad range of assistance strategies. To achieve this goal objects need to be

Figure 1.4: Pedestrians carrying accessories and occlusions complicate the detection task.

detected for a wide range of scales. In particular, when very small objects need to be detected sliding window approaches are a popular choice. They do not rely on the detection of stable keypoint signatures, which tend to diminish at low resolution. In contrast, the object model is learned for a fixed scale and multi-scale detection is achieved by rescaling the input image. However, the choice of the training scale is a difficult design choice to be made. If the scanning window is chosen too small, the learned model will not be able to draw from high resolution evidence and the discriminative power will be low due to a low dimensional representation. This will result in an increased number of false detections. Models learned from a higher resolution at larger training scales will not suffer from this drawback, but will, on the other hand, not be able to detect distant objects on small scales. Figure 1.5 shows street scenes with a large scale range for pedestrians as well as cars.

Figure 1.5: Typical street scenes containing objects with a large scale range. Yellow bounding boxes indicate objects.

Cluttered background. Urban environments offer a high complexity with a wide range of backgrounds (see Figure 1.6). Frequently, structures like street signs or street poles are similar in shape to a pedestrian or a car and lead to false detections. The problem is that object detectors typically only operate on a local sub-window of the entire image. Only when global scene reasoning is employed these false detections can be pruned by exploiting their inconsistency with the rest of the estimated scene.

1.2 CHALLENGES FOR VISUAL SCENE UNDERSTANDING

Figure 1.6: Urban environments are particularly challenging due to cluttered background and distracting background objects.

Difficult lighting and varying appearance. Real-world applications in an outdoor environment naturally suffer from varying lighting due to different weather conditions. While overcast sky results in a diffuse, near uniform lighting, cloudless sky with sunshine causes cast shadows with partially over- and partially under-exposed parts in the image. Under heavily clouded sky as well as at twilight cameras working with visual light tend to under-expose images. Object boundaries diminish and objects do not contrast very well with the background. Further complications arise from rain as wet surfaces change reflectance properties and therefore their visual appearance. Also note that objects appear differently in different lighting. Figure 1.7 shows scenes with difficult weather and lighting conditions.

Figure 1.7: Real-world scenarios need to cope with changing weather and lighting conditions.

Low camera viewpoint and low resolution camera sensors. For mobile platforms, e.g., a robot or a car, a further issue is the relatively low camera viewpoint, which is further complicated by the mostly low resolution cameras used for these applications. This causes the far field to be compressed to only a few pixel lines in the camera's image. When 3D inference is the goal, a slight deviation in detection of a distant object might cause a large error in the estimated 3D position. For instance, given a typical car series camera mounted 1.3 m above ground, 10 meters on the ground plane are projected to 25 pixel rows in 20 meter distance, but to only 3 pixel rows in 70 meters distance. Figure 1.8 plots the number of pixel rows in the image a 10 m stretch on the ground plane projects to depending on the distance to the observer.

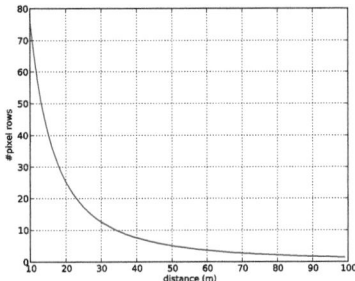

Figure 1.8: Number of image pixel rows a 10m stretch on the ground plane is projected to dependent on the distance from the camera

Local and global information. A further challenge for scene understanding is the gap of locally extracted information to the entire scene's global understanding. Even though objects can be detected relatively reliable by recent methods, usually only a minor part of the image evidence is explored to instantiate an hypothesis. Consequently, false positive detections appear at any scale and position no matter whether they are consistent with other detections or the scene geometry. Several other components of an automotive scene such as forests, bushes, and the street do not have a distinctive common shape and can only be classified locally by their texture (see Figure 1.9 for an illustration). Hence, a major requirement for scene models is the ability to combine the locally extracted evidence efficiently in order to gain global understanding.

Monocular camera. Applications for driver assistance systems frequently use a single monocular camera mounted in the center of the car's windshield. While this enables relatively cheap systems, it complicates the inference of scene depth. This is only possible if further constraints such as a ground plane assumption are employed. Furthermore, we would like to point out that due to the fact that the camera motion is mostly along the camera's optical axis, it is difficult to

1.2 CHALLENGES FOR VISUAL SCENE UNDERSTANDING

Figure 1.9: Locally extracted evidence needs to be put in context to yield global scene understanding. Information gathered from a local patch might not be enough to infer what is observed. For instance, bush and grass on the right might easily be confused.

employ monocular structure from motion methods (Hartley and Zisserman, 2004) as done by other researchers (e.g., Ess et al., 2008). For the far range, stereo image processing is nearly intractable. The camera baseline that is required to observe sufficient disparity exceeds a car's width and is thus hard to realize. Consequently, even when stereo cameras were available, strong appearance models in combination with prior scene knowledge such as presented in this thesis are still required for the far range.

Camera motion. A particular difficulty for moving platforms is the quickly changing background. For many surveillance applications, cameras are mounted fixedly and thus a static background can be assumed. Under these circumstance many systems perform background subtraction (e.g., Stauffer and Grimson, 2000; Elgammal et al., 2000; Sharma and Davis, 2007; Ko et al., 2008) in order to maintain robust object detections. For highly dynamic motion applications such as driver assistance on a highway this is not an option. Here, models need to draw their discriminative power from appearance features. A further restriction arising from highly dynamic motion is motion blur causing a loss of high frequency information. Motion blur heavily affects the close range and makes texture extraction more difficult.

Real-time requirements. Active driver assistance including the control of the car's trajectory in highly dynamic environments requires all sensors to deliver their results at a high frequency. A car driving with a speed of 100 km/h moves 28 meters per second. Even at a sensor frequency of 15 Hz the car will move 1.9 meters while one image frame can be processed. When additional oncoming traffic with similar speed is assumed the cars approach each other 3.8 meters per frame. This exemplifies the need to detect relevant objects as soon as possible and the necessity of a high processing speed to enable quick reactions to critical events.

1.3 CONTRIBUTIONS OF THE THESIS

This thesis builds upon recent work in object detection (Dalal and Triggs, 2005; Dalal et al., 2006) and improves scene segmentation as well as 3D scene understanding by exploiting the position and size of objects like pedestrians and cars in an image. In particular, we shift our focus from detection in photo collections and movies to more realistic real-world onboard scenarios. This thesis contributes three video datasets that are captured from a moving car on highway and in urban environments. By combining object detection with local texture cues we improve performance for the tasks of 2D scene segmentation and 3D scene understanding. In the following, we will discuss our contributions in more detail.

This thesis' technical contributions can be grouped into advances in *people and object detection* and in *scene inference*. We start by discussing our contributions for people and object detection.

Firstly, we conduct an evaluation of static image object descriptors and classifiers for the task of people detection. We show experimentally, that the often employed evaluation in terms of false positive per windows (FPPW) has several shortcomings that may lead to wrong conclusions. Instead we propose to use image based metrics like precision and recall or false positives per image (FPPI). Additionally, we show that a novel descriptor based on the dense sampling of shape context (Belongie et al., 2002) is able to achieve state-of-the-art performance and that the combination of complementary features improves performance.

Secondly, we extend this work to realistic onboard sequences. We show that motion is a helpful cue and allows for performance improvement even for detection from a mobile observer. Moreover, we conduct an extensive study analyzing the performance of several classifiers and show that MPLBoost (Babenko et al., 2008; Kim and Cipolla, 2008) reaches competitive results to SVM based classifiers. Nonetheless, its computational load is substantially lower. Additionally, we contribute a novel training as well as test set containing image pairs to allow for motion descriptors.

Furthermore, we show that modern state-of-the-art object detectors (Dalal and Triggs, 2005) allow for a high degree of parallelization. In a case study we demonstrate that real-time runtime performance can be achieved on recent graphics hardware. However, the concepts we present generalize to other parallel architectures as well. Compared to a CPU implementation we achieve a speed-up of 82 for a pedestrian detector and a speed-up of 53 for a car detector. This implementation has successfully been used for several online demos in projects and has therefore been shown to meet the requirements of mobile platforms.

For the field of global scene inference we contribute two models for the segmentation of 2D images and for inference of the 3D world from a monocular video stream.

Firstly, we present a dynamic CRF model that leverages local texture cues as well as visual object detections to segment an image stream. Long range interactions are introduced by additional nodes, which are instantiated from object detections. We show that this model improves segmentation quality, in particular, for vehicles substantially. Additionally, we show that a dynamic extension over time allows for further performance improvements.

Secondly, we introduce a scene model for monocular 3D understanding of multi-object traffic scenes. Again we leverage segmentation information as well as object detections to gain a symbolic description of the observed scene. The model efficiently exploits prior knowledge and performs joint inference on the camera's pitch as well as on the position and speed of objects. We employ a multi-class object detector and are therefore able to utilize semantic class information. For instance, our dynamic motion model takes advantage of frontal views of objects likely to be oncoming traffic. By jointly inferring the position of all objects we are able to suppress false detections.

1.4 OUTLINE OF THE DOCUMENT

This section gives an overview on the organization of the following chapters. We briefly summarize each chapter and its concepts. Please note that due to project constraints Chapters 3-5 mainly focus on the object class of pedestrians, while Chapter 6 and 7 mainly focus on scene segmentation, vehicle detection and tracking but still employ the same detector.

Chapter 2: Related Work This thesis starts with a broad overview on related research and a discussion on the key differences. We cover the fields of object detection with a focus on methods for pedestrian and vehicle detection, tracking, conditional random field based scene segmentation, and finally scene understanding in 3D as well as in the image domain. For tracking we mostly relate to so called tracking-by-detection methods as these are most relevant to this work.

Chapter 3: Evaluation of Static Features for People Detection In this chapter we provide a performance analysis for several existing and new sliding window based people detectors. This type of object detector is often deployed for automotive and robotics applications for its ability to detect even very small objects. This chapter is motivated by the large number of recently published approaches that either lack an extensive experimental comparison or are hard to reproduce. Often a single feature-classifier combination is evaluated. Here, different features and classifiers are evaluated exhaustively and an overview on the performance of the state-of-the-art in sliding window-based people detection methods is given. We find that the frequently employed false positive per window protocol can fail to predict a detector's true performance for full images. Moreover, we conclude that the combination of complementary features can yield a performance improvement and that a densely sampled shape context descriptor (Belongie et al., 2002) provides similar performance to the very popular histograms of oriented gradients descriptors (Dalal and Triggs, 2005).

The work presented in this chapter corresponds to the DAGM 2008 publication "A Performance Evaluation of Single and Multi-feature People Detection" (Wojek and Schiele, 2008b) and has been extended with Piotr Dollár and Pietro Perona of the Caltech Institute of Technology as a joint CVPR 2009 publication "Pedestrian

Detection: A Benchmark" (Dollár et al., 2009b). It is also part of the broader survey "Visual People Detection: Different Models, Comparison and Discussion" (Schiele et al., 2009). An adapted German translation has appeared in the textbook "Handbuch Fahrerassistenzsysteme" (Schiele and Wojek, 2009).

Chapter 4: Multi-Cue Onboard Pedestrian Detection This chapter extends Chapter 3 to more realistic onboard scenes. Moreover, it does not only analyze static features, but also includes dynamic features, which are derived from optical flow fields. Contrary to the prevalent opinion, we show that motion features can substantially improve detection performance even from a mobile platform. This is in particular true for objects perpendicularly crossing the camera's field of view, which are of great interest to many applications. Additionally, this chapter evaluates four different classifiers AdaBoost, MPLBoost, linear SVM and histogram intersection kernel SVM (HIKSVM). Our experiments indicate that MPLBoost and HIKSVM are the most robust classifiers.

The work presented in this chapter corresponds to another CVPR 2009 publication called "Multi-Cue Onboard Pedestrian Detection" (Wojek et al., 2009).

Chapter 5: Real-Time Object Detection One frequent criticism of sliding window methods is their poor runtime performance making them inappropriate for applications with hard real-time constraints. On the other hand, recent trends in hardware development suggest that modern processing units will not gain further performance by increasing the CPU clock rate but by a higher degree of parallelism with multiple processing units on a single chip. The next chapter will address these issues. We show that the sliding window paradigm offers possibilities of parallelization in both the computation of features and in the evaluation of the classifier. Hence, an adapted implementation can facilitate real-time processing for VGA (640×480 pixel) input streams and scale well to future developments in hardware design.

The work presented in this chapter corresponds to the DAGM 2008 publication "Sliding-Windows for Rapid Object Class Localization: A Parallel Technique" (Wojek et al., 2008). It also appeared in an adapted German translation in the textbook "Handbuch Fahrerassistenzsysteme" (Schiele and Wojek, 2009).

Chapter 6: Dynamic CRFs for Scene Segmentation While Chapters 3-5 were investigating the detection of objects from local evidence in a sliding window framework, this chapter will model objects in their context. In particular, this chapter develops a method to segment a 2D input image stream. It applies a dynamic conditional random field model in order to propagate local neighborhood relations and leverages detections of objects to instantiate long range interactions. By adding these interactions we substantially improve the segmentation of objects compared to segmentation from texture cues only. Further propagating the segmentation over time allows for an additional gain.

The work presented in this chapter corresponds to the ECCV 2008 publication "A

1.4 OUTLINE OF THE DOCUMENT

Dynamic CRF Model for Joint Labeling of Object and Scene Classes" (Wojek and Schiele, 2008a).

Chapter 7: Monocular 3D Scene Modeling and Inference The work in this chapter aims to understand the 3D world from a single monocular stream of 2D images. It employs multi-class object detections and a rough scene segmentation to jointly track the 3D position of objects and the ground plane in a probabilistic model. We show that our scene model is able to outperform several independently working extended Kalman filters and to infer the scene layout robustly up to 100 meters. In particular, performance for small objects in a large distance is improved substantially by our model, which allows to represent inter-object occlusions and object-object interactions.

The work presented in this chapter corresponds to the ECCV 2010 publication "Monocular 3D Scene Modeling and Inference: Understanding Multi-Object Traffic Scenes" (Wojek et al., 2010).

Chapter 8: Conclusion and Future Perspectives The final chapter will conclude this thesis and devise ideas for future research.

RELATED WORK 2

Contents

2.1	Object detection		**16**
	2.1.1	Bottom-up object detection from local evidence	17
	2.1.2	Top-down object detection with global template models	19
	2.1.3	Relation to own work	27
2.2	2D context and semantic scene labeling		**28**
	2.2.1	Object detection in 2D context	28
	2.2.2	Semantic scene labeling	29
	2.2.3	Relation to own work	32
2.3	Tracking		**33**
	2.3.1	Relation to own work	36
2.4	3D scene understanding		**37**
	2.4.1	Relation to own work	40

EVER since the field emerged, automatic scene understanding from still images and videos has been investigated in the computer vision literature. Early approaches (for surveys see Binford, 1982; Tsotsos, 1987) in the 1960s and 1970s mostly used geometric and symbolic approaches. Often these were limited to handle unrealistic data due to the limited robustness with respect to difficult background clutter. Moreover, many models were based on heuristics and did not allow to cover the variability of real world problems.

Probabilistic and statistical learning methods (e.g., Bishop, 2006; Friedman *et al.*, 2000; Schoelkopf and Smola, 2001) developed within the last 20 years address many of the field's early problems. As a consequence previously unsolvable problems seem to come into reach again. Among those are the robust and reliable detection of previously unseen objects and the automatic analysis and understanding of entire scenes, which are both in the focus of this thesis.

In particular within the last few years, the corpus of related work has become abundant. Hence, our chapter on related work is mostly focusing on seminal work on the following directly related tasks of our work:

- Object detection
- 2D context and semantic scene labeling
- Tracking
- 3D scene understanding

With *object detection* we refer to methods that aim to detect *any* previously unseen object instance of a certain class. Detection typically includes the (x,y)-position within the image as well as the object's size which is usually returned as scale with respect to the object model. In particular, we are interested to automatically learn object models (i.e., fit model parameters) from training data with machine learning methods. Our focus is on supervised learning methods and therefore the training data is assumed to include labels denoting the training instances' position and size. As our work is applied in robotics and automotive scenarios, the main objects of interest are vehicles and pedestrians. However, we emphasize that the models developed in this thesis are in general applicable to other object classes as well.

We subsume methods that aim at improving object detection by global image models under object detection in *2D context*. In this group of related work, methods typically employ context on the object level, e.g., global co-occurrence statistics. *Semantic scene labeling* denotes the task to label every pixel of an previously unobserved input image with the displayed object or scene class. Our work considers in particular highway and urban road scenes that are recorded from an onboard camera. Like for object detection we focus on methods that are able to learn an appearance model for every class label from pixel-wise labeled training data. We will also review models that model the neighborhood (e.g., by CRFs) of a classified pixel. According to Divvala et al. (2009) this type of context can be referred to as *2D scene gist context* when features are derived from the full image or as *semantic context* when the relationship among object classes is modeled.

By *tracking* we mean to repeatedly identify an entity (e.g., an object hypothesis) over longer periods of time across multiple frames. Typical tracking approaches consist of the association strategy which links the entities and a dynamic model which captures the expected dynamics. Thus, information of nearby frames contributes to the *temporal context*.

Finally, we review related work on *3D scene understanding* which leverages *3D scene context* in order to infer a scene's 3D layout. Due to this task's complexity, related work is mostly described in the literature of entire vision systems. However, we will also point to notable exceptions. These include approaches to infer scene properties from low-level features without the notion of an semantic object class such as surface orientation or depth from monocular images.

In the following each of the above tasks is reviewed separately with focus on robotics and automotive applications. We conclude each section by setting our own work in relation to previous work on the discussed task.

2.1 OBJECT DETECTION

We begin by summarizing related work in the field of object detection for which several different types of approaches exist. In this section we will distinguish bottom-up approaches which accumulate local evidence to form object hypotheses and top-down approaches which generate hypotheses by matching a global object model.

We will focus on approaches that are in general applicable to any object class, but note that more specialized detectors also exist. These explicitly exploit object class specific properties as for instance cast shadows below vehicles for vehicle detection. Some of these methods are covered in two recent surveys on on-road vehicle detection

2.1 OBJECT DETECTION

(Sun *et al.*, 2006) and on pedestrian detection (Geronimo *et al.*, 2009).

We will briefly review bottom-up object detection approaches in Section 2.1.1 and then give a thorough survey in section Section 2.1.2 on pedestrian and object detection approaches with global models. As discussed before the latter are more relevant to our work.

2.1.1 Bottom-up object detection from local evidence

Body plans. Forsyth and Fleck (1997) propose to approximate objects as an assembly of cylinders. Evidence is aggregated in a hierarchical bottom-up fashion by first fitting cylinders to the image's segmentation and then grouping pairs of cylinders. On higher levels the groups of lower hierarchy levels are fused to incrementally obtain an object hypothesis on the top node.

This work has been extended by Ioffe and Forsyth (2001). Here human body parts are detected by a segment detector which responds to parallel lines. AdaBoost (Friedman *et al.*, 2000) is employed to learn kinematic constraints and group single segments in a bottom-up fashion. While the kinematic model is able to prune many false segment detections, the segment detection stage is rather limited. Only persons wearing a bathing suit are detected in front of uncluttered background.

Pictorial structures. Another prominent model is the pictorial structures model which dates back to Fischler and Elschlager (1973). It models object parts with kinematic constraints in a deformable tree-structured model and requires the parts to be detected with a confidence estimate. Gaussian distributions model the parts' displacement. An efficient inference method based on convolution for sum-product inference or generalized distance transform for max-product inference is proposed by Felzenszwalb and Huttenlocher (2000). Andriluka *et al.* (2009) show that with a powerful part detector based on AdaBoost and shape context (Belongie *et al.*, 2002) as dense feature descriptor can yield promising results for pedestrian detection as well as for 2D body pose estimation.

Constellation model. Among others Weber *et al.* (2000) and Fergus *et al.* (2007) propose to model the relations of parts in terms of a constellation model. For this model distinctive object parts are automatically extracted and the most discriminative parts' constellation is assumed to follow a mixture of Gaussians distribution. The model parameters are learned in an unsupervised fashion with an expectation-maximization (EM) algorithm (Dempster *et al.*, 1977). Weber *et al.* (2000) extract part candidates with a Förstner interest point operator (Förstner and Gülch, 1987) and obtain a vocabulary of distinctive parts by k-Means clustering. A cross-validation scheme is applied during the training procedure to further reduce the number of parts which are represented. The model's main limitation is its inability to handle a large number of parts (>10 parts) due to the exponential growth of possible constellations. Fergus *et al.* (2007) enhance this model by taking shape, appearance, occlusion and relative scale into account. Moreover, an entropy-based feature detector (Kadir and Brady, 2001) produces more stable interest points. Convincing results are shown for the classification of cars as well as faces. Stark et al. (2009) apply the constellation model to detect shape classes. They use k-adjacent segments (Ferrari et al., 2008) as parts and adopt a MCMC scheme for inference in order to reduce the computational complexity.

Discriminative methods. Agarwal et al. (2004) propose a vocabulary based approach. Parts are learned in a preprocessing step by clustering image patches gathered from keypoint responses (Förstner and Gülch, 1987). At training time all patches on the training image are matched to the vocabulary clusters (the codebook) based on normalized correlation. A classifier, which is learned from the distances on the scale normalized training images, models the matched parts' pairwise relation. Testing is performed in a sliding window fashion. Experiments are conducted on the UIUC side-view car dataset which contains realistic images with moderate background clutter. This paper is also one of the first works that introduces image-based evaluation metrics and emphasizes the importance of consistent evaluation. In particular this paper suggests the performance metrics precision, recall and the F-measure.

Mikolajczyk et al. (2004) exploit discriminative part detectors for face and human detection. These detectors employ gradient orientations as features and the AdaBoost framework for classification. The appearance of 7 individual parts is learned from training samples. To allow multi-scale detection parts are first detected by a sliding window approach and responses are combined in a bottom-up process. This process is anchored on successfully detected parts and models the spatial relation of parts by means of Gaussian distributions which are learned from training data. This model has successfully been applied to faces seen from multiple viewpoints and to human detection. The experiments show that probabilistic part combination is able to significantly reduce the number of false positives of stand-alone part detectors.

Implicit shape model. Leibe et al. (2008a) propose the implicit shape model (ISM). In this work a star model represents the spatial distribution of parts with respect to the object, while the vocabulary of object parts is learned similarly to Agarwal et al. (2004). A 3D Hough voting space in position and scale is exploited for inference. Object hypotheses are found as local modes in the voting space by mean-shift search. Furthermore, a maximum description length (MDL) formulation is used in order to obtain the optimal assignment of parts to object hypotheses. Additionally, this model allows to obtain an object segmentation by back-projection of the contributing parts' segmentation. Leibe et al. (2005) apply this model to pedestrians in crowded scenes and achieve additional robustness with a global model verification step based on Chamfer distances (Borgefors, 1988).

Seemann et al. (2005) conduct an extensive study on different feature descriptors to optimize the local representation and found shape context (Belongie et al., 2002) to work best. Seemann et al. (2006) and Seemann and Schiele (2006) propose further extensions for multi-aspect people detection and cross-articulation learning. Mikolajczyk et al. (2006) present an extension to multi-class detection with this generative model. This work exploits a hierarchical ball tree data structure for efficient feature matching and allows in-plane rotation-invariant detection of side-view cars, motorbikes, bikes, pedestrians and RPG shooters on realistic images. Maji and Malik (2009) present an extension to the ISM model that learns the parts' Hough voting weights discriminativly in a max-margin framework.

Conditional random fields. Conditional Random Fields (CRFs) have recently been applied to model object classes. Quattoni et al. (2007) use a keypoint detector to determine object parts which are described by SIFT features (Lowe, 2004). A minimum spanning tree connects the n-nearest parts for each keypoint. Inference with belief propagation determines whether the sliding window is showing an object instance or background. In this model parts are not spatially localized and moreover, the parts' latent variables are connected to their nearest neighbors only. Hence, long-range interactions are not well modeled in this work.

To mitigate this shortcoming Kapoor and Winn (2006) propose an additional latent variable connected to all parts which allows a tighter variable coupling. Moreover, their model enforces a spatial localization of object parts. Both works conduct experiments on side-view cars introduced by Agarwal and Roth (2002) and show state-of-the-art performance. Both CRF models are able to handle single object instances, but do not account for object occlusion. Winn and Shotton (2006) address inter-object occlusion with a layout consistent CRF. They propose an expansion move algorithm for efficient inference and show semantic object segmentation despite occlusion for cars as well as faces. A further extension (Hoiem et al., 2007b) uses a 3D model during training and presents results on even more complex images of cars taken from the PASCAL image dataset (Everingham et al., 2010).

Schnitzspan et al. (2008) present a similar model to Winn and Shotton (2006) that exploits a hierarchical CRF structure with three layers to combine object descriptions of different granularity on local, semi-global and global scale. State-of-the-art performance is demonstrated for motorbikes. Further extensions perform structure learning (Schnitzspan et al., 2009) and learn semantically meaningful parts (Schnitzspan et al., 2010).

A major drawback of the above CRF models is their computational complexity, which is currently prohibitive for realistic applications. Moreover, these models do not allow to model object scale easily. Thus, they usually conduct inference by scanning the entire scale range or exploit another object detector to generate regions of interest with a high recall in a preprocessing step.

2.1.2 Top-down object detection with global template models

The second group of related algorithms we discuss is based on the principle of template matching which became increasingly popular as modern machine learning methods evolved within the last few years. These detection approaches typically model the object to be detected with a global description within a scale and position normalized window and use a discriminative classifier to determine positive and negative instances. These methods commonly assume that a sufficient amount of labeled training data is available in order to provide sufficient statistics to fit the model parameters. To localize objects in unseen images during test time most approaches adopt a sliding window approach, i.e., the model is evaluated for densely sampled image positions and scales. As the classifier usually responds to multiple nearby windows per object instance, a non-maximum suppression step to fuse nearby detections needs to be applied for post-processing.

To map a classified window's image content to appropriate feature spaces, a number of different descriptors have been proposed in the literature. Some of the desired feature space properties are invariance to varying illumination, a low dimensional representation to allow efficient training methods and invariance to intra-class and pose variation. And most importantly, good feature spaces have to allow a good separability of positive and negative samples with the deployed classification framework.

Wavelet-based descriptors. One popular approach to model the statistics of objects are wavelets. Papageorgiou and Poggio (2000) propose to employ an over-complete set of horizontal, vertical and diagonal Haar wavelet basis functions to model objects. The representation is extracted at two different scales. As classifier a support vector machine (SVM) with a quadratic kernel is deployed. This approach has successfully been used even in the presence of substantial background clutter for several classes including faces, cars and pedestrians. Even real-time performance within a full detection system is possible when the model is restricted to hand marked discriminative window regions.

Viola and Jones (2004) extend this work in several aspects. Firstly, they generalize Haar basis functions to the more general and powerful set of Haar-like features. Secondly, they use AdaBoost to select discriminative features instead of hand labeling discriminative window regions. To achieve real-time performance, they pursue a classifier cascade strategy in order to quickly discard windows that are unlikely to contain an object. Convincing results for this approach are presented for the class of faces.

Similarly, Schneiderman and Kanade (2004) use histograms on wavelet filter bank coefficients in order to describe cars and faces from multiple viewpoints. AdaBoost is employed as classification framework. In order to handle multiple viewpoints this paper trains several models and returns the viewpoint of the model with the strongest response.

Gradient-based descriptors. The success of wavelets in the above works relied to a large extent on the normalization of the wavelet responses to achieve invariance towards changes in lighting. Often however, gradients allow a more robust object description. Shashua *et al.* (2004) propose localized parts described with histograms of gradients to model pedestrians. They deploy a two-stage classification system for classification and evaluate the detector within a complete automotive system. To cope with different viewpoints the training data is clustered and per cluster a different discriminative classifier is trained. On the second classification stage AdaBoost is used to fuse the parts' classification results. As a stereo setup is employed to generate regions of interest it is hard to assess the detector's stand-alone performance from this work.

Similarly, Soga *et al.* (2005) and Zhao and Thorpe (2000) propose detection systems that exploit low-level stereo information to instantiate regions of interest but use gradients to describe pedestrians. Soga *et al.* (2005) employ gradients in four directions as features in an SVM, while Zhao and Thorpe (2000) deploy a neural network on the gradients' magnitudes for classification.

Another very successful approach for pedestrian detection has been developed by Dalal and Triggs (2005). Inspired by the scale-invariant feature transform (SIFT, Lowe, 2004) objects are represented by histograms of oriented gradients (HOG). Robustness with respect to lighting is achieved by local histogram normalization. More specific, HOG cells describe object classes locally by tri-linearly (with respect to direction and position) interpolated histograms on gradient orientation. Cells are normalized with respect to different neighborhoods in blocks of 2×2 cells. For classification an SVM classifier is deployed. As this description results in a high dimensional feature space, a sufficient amount of training data is required to cover the intra-class variability of pedestrians.

To mitigate this drawback Fritz and Schiele (2008) propose to exploit an intermediate representation which is obtained by a topic model. Their work suggest to use the LDA model (Griffiths and Steyvers, 2004) to infer co-occurring gradient orientations. Experiments convincingly show that the number of training samples can be substantially reduced without a loss in detection performance. Bissacco *et al.* (2006) exploit a similar model for pedestrian detection and additionally retrieve the detected humans' pose by finding the nearest neighbor in the lower dimensional topic space. Results for pose estimation are, however, only presented on motion capture data recorded in lab environments. Thus, it is unclear how well this approach performs for realistic environments.

Laptev (2006) integrates histograms on gradients with AdaBoost as classifier. Contrary to most other work, this paper defines the weak learners on entire histograms and not only on the feature vector's single entries. Histograms are mapped to a scalar value by means of a weighted Fischer linear discriminant (Fisher, 1936). Hence, weak learners are more powerful and compared to other approaches a stronger classifier is obtained with an equal number of stages. This method reports results for the PASCAL 2005 dataset for people, bicycles, motorbikes and cars and outperforms the best challenge entries.

Maji *et al.* (2008) exploit a pyramid representation to describe humans with varying granularity and use differently sized cells for their histograms of gradient orientations. Additionally, they propose an approximation to the histogram intersection kernel for SVMs. This approximation allows a substantial speed-up and thus enables a kernel SVM to be used for sliding window detection. Most other work often uses a pre-filtering step with computationally cheaper classifiers or relies on linear SVMs with a more powerful and discriminative feature representation.

Contrary to many others, who use histograms to represent an object's statistics, Tuzel *et al.* (2008) suggest to use covariance matrices on the distribution of raw features. These covariance matrices are computed on local sub-windows. As raw features image gradients' orientation and magnitude and the image intensity's second derivatives are used. Since covariance matrices do not lie on a vector space, the LogitBoost classification framework is modified to work on Riemannian manifolds with improved performance. Convincing results are presented for the detection of humans on the challenging INRIA

Person (Dalal and Triggs, 2005) database.

Liu et al. (2009) propose the concept of granularity-tunable gradient partitions. Their idea is to represent objects at different levels of granularity ranging from a statistic representation such as a histogram to a deterministic representation such as a gradient image. Dollár et al. (2007) propose to learn an appropriate representation by *feature mining*. They compute Haar wavelet responses on several channels as candidate features for their AdaBoost framework. Compared to other work feature selection from a large pool of possible features is improved. The idea is to start with a set of randomly selected features and apply a steepest descent method for the best candidate to further optimize the weak learner's discriminative power. This method outperforms several other methods on the DaimlerChrysler classification dataset (Munder and Gavrila, 2006).

Shape-based description. Despite an object's appearance, shape is frequently used as a feature for object detection. In particular for pedestrian detection, it has been argued that shape is one of the most promising cues. Gavrila and Philomin (1999) match pedestrians' shape on the input image by a hierarchical matching strategy. During testing the Hausdorff distance transform allows to quickly compute the template's and image's similarity. Broggi et al. (2000) assume vertical symmetry for pedestrians to describe their shape. However, to achieve robustness their system relies on a stereo post-processing step to filter false positives.

While the two previous methods model a pedestrian's shape globally, other approaches model the shape only locally. Wu and Nevatia (2005) use edgelets to detect head, upper body and legs as well as the full body. A joint likelihood map for all objects within an image is used to combine these part detectors. Joint reasoning allows to explain missing parts which arise from inter-object occlusion. However, this pedestrian detector is restricted to front or back views. Thus, this work has been extended by Wu and Nevatia (2007a) to handle multiple viewpoints. A tree-structured classifier scheme with AdaBoost classifiers is proposed. Discriminative features are used to cluster the data in an unsupervised way during the training procedure. State-of-the-art detection results are presented for multi-view pedestrian and car detection.

Sabzmeydani and Mori (2007) propose to directly learn shape features from gradient responses. Their approach suggests a two-level AdaBoost hierarchy, where the first layer classifies the pedestrian shape locally and the second layer combines the first level classifier output. Lin and Davis (2008) use a part-template tree model to model a pedestrian's shape locally for head, upper body and legs and extract HOG appearance descriptors along the shape's outline. It is worth noting, that in this approach the inferred shape is only used to determine where to extract the appearance descriptor in the sliding window.

Stereo-based descriptors. Even though several systems such as proposed by Shashua et al. (2004) or Gavrila and Munder (2007) employ disparity information to generate regions of interest in order to reduce the runtime of their detection step, only few approaches have directly used disparity features for sliding window classification. A high level fusion scheme is proposed by Rohrbach et al. (2009). Their detector independently classifies a bounding box based on intensity or disparity information and fuses both by employing an SVM with a Gaussian kernel. The authors also investigate models in the joint feature space but found them to perform less well.

Hattori et al. (2009) also explore two different integration schemes. First, stereo is used to associate a bounding box of the left view with a bounding box on the right view. Both views are individually classified based on intensity and the classifier output is combined to obtain the final classification score. Second, new descriptors which are inspired by HOG (Dalal and Triggs, 2005) are designed to model disparity statistics. Experiments in real world urban sequences show that both schemes improve false positive rate without impact on the detection rate.

Rapus et al. (2008) investigate recently developed low-resolution time-of-flight and intensity cameras for pedestrian detection. In their approach depth information is first exploited to estimate a ground plane. The according ground plane region is considered as background and removed from the depth image and the remaining foreground regions are scanned. Despite the low resolution this detection system achieves 80% recall (on pedestrians up to 20 m). It will be interesting to see in the future how improvements on the hardware with respect to resolution will impact the detection performance.

Motion-based descriptors. According to psychologists and neuroscientists motion is an important cue for the human object perception. Nonetheless, only few computer vision object detectors make use of motion features. For moving cameras as in our work, it is often argued that the camera's ego-motion impedes performance improvements. Wöhler and Anlauf (1999) exploit artificial neural networks with gray scale images as input to model pedestrians. A layered hierarchy termed local receptive fields is developed and trained with the well-known backpropagation algorithm. A time-delayed neural network architecture further allows to process image sequences. From the provided experiments it is unclear, how well this architecture is suited when the camera itself undergoes severe ego-motion.

In an extension to Viola and Jones (2004), Viola et al. (2005) suggest to compute wavelet features on difference images. Their experiments are conducted in an surveillance environment with static cameras. Thus, their method is only applicable to moving cameras when the input images are (at least approximately) ego-motion compensated. As this is a non-trivial task, Dalal et al. (2006) model motion statistics based on the optic flow field's internal differences. Therefore, uniform image motion is compensated locally. While they found an improvement compared to their static image detector with an evaluation on single bounding boxes in terms of false positives per window, Dalal (2006) only reports performance on-par compared to Dalal and Triggs (2005) for a full image-based evaluation.

Enzweiler et al. (2008) propose an attention mechanism to generate regions of interest based on optic flow. The camera's ego-motion is corrected explicitly and performance is evaluated for the entire system. The experiments indicate that system performance can be improved as fewer false regions of interest are generated.

Infrared imaging. Infrared cameras provide a technically complementary sensor modality to visual light sensors. Currently, they are often deployed in nighttime pedestrian detection systems for their ability to sense warmth. Xu et al. (2005) for instance present a system based on hot-spot detection which aims to detect heads and hands. In a second step these candidates are verified with a full-body detector based on raw infrared image intensity. Bertozzi et al. (2007) demonstrate a system that is working on far-infrared (FIR) stereo images. Detection consists of three modules to achieve robustness under various environment conditions including sunny summer days when pedestrians and the background environment emit similar heat signatures. These modules are warm area detection, vertical edge detection and stereo disparity matching.

Motivated by the success for visual light cameras several approaches have been adapted to infrared cameras. Histograms of oriented gradients on infrared images, for instance, are investigated by Suard et al. (2006). Mählisch et al. (2005) evaluate hierarchical Chamfer matching and detection with Haar-like wavelet cascades (Viola and Jones, 2004).

However, little research is available to assess and compare the applicability for daytime applications. A notable exception are Krotosky and Trivedi (2007), who compare visual light color cameras with infrared imaging devices. Even though the experiments shown are limited to a single scene without a thorough quantitative evaluation, the authors conclude that sensor fusion might be beneficial. To this end further research on much larger datasets is required.

Feature combination. So far, we discussed approaches that employ a single feature type for object representation. However, not all features model the same object properties and hence these representations are partially complementary. Multi-feature or cue combination approaches aim to exploit this fact in order to achieve improved performance. Among them are hierarchical classification frameworks, joint feature spaces as well as cascaded classifiers. The latter is for instance used by Gavrila and Munder (2007). Shape based detections are first verified by a texture classifier and by a stereo verification step. Both verification steps prove effective to improve performance.

Schwartz et al. (2009) employ a high dimensional feature space ($\approx$170,000 dimensions) to represent pedestrians by their edges, texture and color. Partial least square analysis discovers feature correlations during training. These are used to project the representation in a lower dimensional feature space. Dollár et al. (2009a) improve Dollár et al. (2007) with a generalized notion of integral channel features. Compared to their earlier work, a larger number of input channels including edge and color channels are used. This paper shows that normalized color channels such as LUV can be beneficial for pedestrian detection. The method presented is currently one of the top-performing methods for pedestrian detection.

Vedaldi et al. (2009) propose a detection system that learns feature combination weights by means of multiple kernel learning. Due to its high computational complexity several approximations are proposed for this approach to allow efficient inference. This method achieves state-of-the-art performance for several object classes on the PASCAL 2009 dataset. Wu and Nevatia (2008) automatically learn the efficiency-

2.1 OBJECT DETECTION

discriminance trade-off in a boosting cascade for HOG, edgelet and covariance features with a focus on runtime. Nonetheless, this approach outperforms the three stand-alone single cue detectors. This is surprising in that even three gradient based features contain complementary information due to different means of modeling the distribution.

Wang et al. (2009) combine HOG with a texture description based on local binary patterns (Ojala et al., 2002). Additionally, a linear SVM classifier is modified to automatically perform partial occlusion reasoning. Color information and implicit segmentation is added to the successful HOG feature by Ott and Everingham (2009). They report a performance improvement compared to pure HOG detection for pedestrians as well as for person, bus and sheep detection on the PASCAL dataset. Walk et al. (2010) propose to combine a number of different features including HOG, a motion descriptor and a feature describing the local self-similarity of pedestrians. Thus, this approach leverages multiple sources of complementary information and is currently among the state-of-the-art methods for pedestrian detection for onboard applications.

Flexible part-based approaches. In particular for the detection of humans the notion of flexible parts is investigated to cope with the high degree of articulation. While bottom-up detection strategies mostly have an inherent notion of parts, it is more difficult to include this notion in top-down template matching approaches. However, several works have successfully managed this.

Among them are Mohan et al. (2001), who successfully extend the work by Papageorgiou and Poggio (2000). They propose a two stage SVM approach. In the first stage head, arms and legs are detected and verified to fit a rough geometric constellation. The second stage fuses the first stage's classification scores to obtain a detection window's final confidence.

Tran and Forsyth (2008) jointly learn body pose estimation and person classification. In a fully supervised setting this task is formulated as a structured learning problem. An structured output SVM (Taskar et al., 2005) is trained to classify each bounding box into person or non-person and at the same time the joints' positions are retrieved. While this paper shows state-of-the-art detection performance, the accuracy of the body pose estimate is only visualized in some samples.

Dollár et al. (2008) employ multi-instance learning in order to automatically determine the position of parts during learning. Classification confidence on the part level is fed into an AdaBoost framework to yield a confidence on the window level. This method obtains state-of-the-art performance on the INRIA Person dataset and has been refined by Lin et al. (2009), who propose a more efficient training procedure.

Felzenszwalb et al. (2008) propose a part-based approach employing a latent SVM which models the unknown part positions as latent variables. Felzenszwalb et al. (2009) reformulate this approach as an multi-instance learning problem. Additionally, this work introduces mixture distributions for parts to model several poses and articulations for an object class. This approach yields state-of-the-art performance on several PASCAL datasets and also for people and pedestrian detection.

Performance evaluations. Unified evaluation criteria and a consistent experimental protocol are essential to obtain a fair comparison for different approaches. As the above section shows, within the last years the number of published approaches to object detection constantly grew. However, only few works evaluate with a consistent protocol on the same datasets. Additionally, many methods only deploy a single classifier or a certain feature while other combinations are often not considered. A thorough evaluation evaluates all combinations exhaustively to gain insights into the learning method as well as into feature design.

Munder and Gavrila (2006) publish a gray scale dataset consisting of several thousand pedestrian and non-pedestrian crops with a size of 18×36 pixel. Haar wavelets (Viola and Jones, 2004), local receptive fields (Wöhler and Anlauf, 1999) and PCA coefficients are evaluated in combination with neural networks and SVMs with different kernels. This study finds local receptive fields in combination with a quadratic SVM to work best. As this dataset consists of crops only, the according evaluation is limited to single window classification.

A more recent survey by Enzweiler and Gavrila (2009) analyzes the performance of HOG features, Haar wavelets and local receptive fields not only for stand-alone detection but also in a real-time system with limited processing capabilities. They find HOG descriptors with a linear SVM to work best; both as stand-alone detector as well as in a system with low temporal constraints. When temporal constraints are increased to real-time requirements of automotive systems this works reports the Viola-Jones cascade detector (Viola and Jones, 2004) to work best.

Dollár et al. (2009b) propose a new dataset along with an extensive study of current state-of-the-art methods. Compared to most previous work this dataset is by the order of an magnitude larger and the original authors' implementations are used to ensure the original methods from the literature are reproduced accurately. This paper discusses different evaluation methodologies and suggests (similarly to Agarwal et al., 2004) to use image based metrics in order to assess not only the detector's classification part in isolation but also essential post-processing steps such as non-maximum suppression.

Real-time implementations. In order to achieve real-time performance several applications demand frame rates as high as 20 Hz. To achieve this runtime performance two strategies or a mixture of both are currently investigated. Firstly, well performing methods are approximated while mostly detection performance is sacrificed. Zhu et al. (2006) approximate HOG by omitting Gaussian weighting with respect to the pixel position within a block. This allows to leverage fast integral histogram methods (Porikli, 2005). In combination with an AdaBoost cascade for classification their approach achieves real-time performance with almost no loss in detection accuracy. However, this approach might not achieve very high speed-ups for detection on small scales. Zhang et al. (2007) propose a coarse to fine scanning method. The input image is first rescaled to a smaller size and tested with an inaccurate and lower dimensional but fast model. Selected candidates are tested with a high resolution model on the original image scale. While this method allows speed-ups for relatively large objects it does not allow to accelerate small scale object detection.

2.1 OBJECT DETECTION

And secondly, other works propose to parallelize algorithms in order to run them on specialized hardware (e.g., GPUs). Recent trends in hardware development show, that future computers will not increase computational power by higher clock rates but by massive parallelism. Thus, even though hardware platforms are likely to change in the future, this approach is appealing nonetheless. Zhang and Nevatia (2008) and Prisacariu and Reid (2009) follow this approach by employing massively parallel graphics co-processors in order to implement the popular HOG detection approach in real-time.

2.1.3 Relation to own work

The work in this thesis has been inspired by Dalal and Triggs (2005) and Dalal et al. (2006). Dense features based on gradient statistics have in recent literature shown to be very robust even for detection of very small objects. This is crucial for our work as application-relevant objects recorded by automotive onboard cameras appear at object sizes as small as 20 pixels. As most work only considers a specific combination of features and classifiers for their detection system, we perform a rigorous evaluation in Chapter 3 which exhaustively evaluates all combinations for recently proposed features and classifiers for people detection. This evaluation and its extension in Dollár et al. (2009b) also revealed that some recent methods over-reported performance with the false positive per window metric which could not be reproduced when single window classifiers were run in a full detector setting. Therefore, we argue in this work contrary to many others to use full image based metrics for detector evaluation.

Similar to other work (Gavrila and Munder, 2007; Dalal et al., 2006) we investigate multi-feature and cue combination. While Dalal et al. (2006) and Viola et al. (2005) have proposed methods to exploit motion features, they were restricted to rather low dynamic movies and to a surveillance scenario. In Chapter 4 we continue the evaluation of Chapter 3 but include motion features and focus on onboard scenarios, for which motion was previously rarely exploited as a cue. Moreover, we detail several crucial implementation details which are often overseen in related work which mostly focuses on features and classifier learning. We find that in a full detector system pre- and post-processing like non-maximum suppression also need careful consideration to achieve best performance. Only with these crucial details we are able to obtain improved performance with a motion-enhanced detector. With MPLBoost we investigate a classifier that is more robust to changes in viewpoint and articulation than the popular AdaBoost framework. The MPLBoost framework performs clustering on discriminative features while a strong classifier is trained. This is contrary to others, who often perform offline clustering or explicitly label viewpoints to separate the training data (Shashua et al., 2004; Gavrila and Philomin, 1999).

While several fast approximation methods were proposed to achieve real-time performance with successful detection frameworks, these often come at the price of a loss in detection performance (Zhu et al., 2006; Zhang et al., 2007). In Chapter 5 we argue that massive parallelism of today's hardware can better be exploited to satisfy real-time constraints while maintaining detection performance.

2.2 2D CONTEXT AND SEMANTIC SCENE LABELING

We continue with the description of related work for object detection in 2D context and semantic scene labeling. Approaches for object detection in 2D context typically infer object positions in 2D image coordinates supported by the semantic context of other objects, without segmenting or labeling the full scene. Semantic scene labeling typically aims to infer an object or background scene class for all pixels or for larger regions (e.g., super-pixels; Shi and Malik, 2000; Felzenszwalb and Huttenlocher., 2004) supported by the local image neighborhood. As inference from the local image content is limited many models make use of semantic context and combine the local inference results in a global model. For this task CRFs (Lafferty *et al.*, 2001) are frequently applied.

2.2.1 Object detection in 2D context

Scene context. As discussed in Section 2.1 bottom-up as well as top-down methods for object detection only use a local neighborhood in the image x-y-scale space to instantiate an object hypothesis. The single hypotheses' relation with respect to each other or with respect to the overall scene are usually neglected. Torralba (2003) uses the global statistics of a low-level Gabor filter bank to estimate an a-priori likelihood on possible object positions within an image by a mixture of Gaussians. This paper also proposes to perform scale selection from global image features and shows results on a dataset consisting of a large variety of scenes. A more integrated approach is presented by Murphy *et al.* (2003). This work proposes a conditional random field model to jointly classify scenes and detect objects. It uses local features to instantiate object hypotheses with a sliding window object detector and global gist features to describe the scene.

Tu *et al.* (2005) employ Markov chain Monte Carlo (MCMC) sampling to obtain a hierarchical representation of an image. They construct a parsing graph for the global scene by maximizing a generative model and employ bottom-up discriminative object detectors to dynamically reconfigure this graph and explore high-density regions of the generative model. Similarly, Heitz and Koller (2008) employ Gibbs sampling for inference to combine region segmentation (stuff) with the presence of objects (things). Their things and stuff model, an instance of a Markov random field (MRF), is able to model different relations such as "a region with a certain texture appears above an object" or "an object appears on a region with a certain color".

Lampert and Blaschko (2008) propose to model object class co-occurrence within an image with a multiple kernel learning approach, while Gallagher and Chen (2009) propose to leverage social context to improve image understanding with groups of people. Their model not only infers the position of faces, but also gender, age, camera position and the image's event type.

Detector context. While many contextual models on object level expect object hypotheses as input, Fink and Perona (2003) design object detectors that already learn contextual models within the detection stage. They simultaneously learn object detectors

2.2 2D CONTEXT AND SEMANTIC SCENE LABELING

for several classes and incorporate context into AdaBoost's weak learners. Contrary to the standard formulation not only image-based weak learners are examined during learning. All detectors' confidence from previous stages in a local neighborhood is additionally considered as feature for a weak learner. Kruppa and Schiele (2003) extend Schneiderman and Kanade (2004) and show that improved detection performance can be achieved when local context information is included in the detection framework. In particular they show that face detection can be supported by an extended detector which also models neck and shoulder. A performance improvement is in particular achieved for objects on small scales.

2.2.2 Semantic scene labeling

Single-layer approaches. Semantic scene labeling has been researched in the computer vision community since several years. While current approaches resort to probabilistic modeling early approaches tried rule-based reasoning with some success. SCHEMA for instance is one of the early systems proposed by Draper *et al.* (1989). They employ bottom-up grouping of so called tokens to obtain a segmentation of input images. Their results are however only limited to some sample images and it is hard to estimate how well this system works for general scenes.

More recent approaches typically start from extracting local statistics to obtain a local class estimate. Vogel and Schiele (2007) for instance classify scenes but use local semantically meaningful classes on a grid as intermediate representation. They use a multi-cue representation containing color as well as edge statistics in order to obtain classes such as grass, field, sand, foliage, water or rocks. Starting with Kumar and Hebert (2003), who label man-made structures and background, CRFs are frequently used for semantic scene labeling. Additional to local (unary) classification, these models allow interaction with neighboring regions and thus a global reasoning.

While Kumar and Hebert (2003) compute their local statistics on a regular lattice structure, Carbonetto *et al.* (2004) also compare regular grids to regions of an image's over-segmentation obtained by NCut (Shi and Malik, 2000). Additionally, their model uses word annotations. This paper concludes that spatial context modeling by means of pairwise interaction potentials is more important than the underlying initial segmentation. The experimental results indicate roughly equal performance for a regular grid structure and for NCut over-segmentation.

Turtinen and Pietikäinen (2006) employ texture features (Ojala *et al.*, 2002) together with an SVM for local classification on the OUTEX outdoor texture database. To model neighborhood relations on a grid structure a CRF framework is employed and edge potentials are learned from training data. While the CRF model substantially improves the local patch classification, it remains unclear how well this model performs on more realistic scenes which not only contain textured regions but also objects.

Shotton *et al.* (2009) apply the CRF framework for image segmentation with 21 scene and object classes. Several cues including texture, color and location are fused. Due to the large number of parameters to be fitted in this model, standard learning methods yield unsatisfying results. The paper instead proposes a piecewise approach to learn the edge potentials' factors individually.

Rabinovich et al. (2007) exploit semantic context based on stable over-segmentations. As these over-segmentations usually contain few regions, a dense CRF graph structure over all segments is feasible for inference. Context knowledge is obtained from two sources: (1) from the co-occurrence in training images and (2) from the internet source Google sets. Both sources allow to improve the individual region classification that is based on a bag-of-words representation.

As frequently used filter bank features and CRF inference are often criticized as slow, Shotton et al. (2008) propose semantic texton forests which directly use pixel intensity values as input and omit the feature computation stage. Instead of CRFs a image-level prior distribution gained from global image categorization is employed for semantic context modeling. Schroff et al. (2008) use random forests with a large number of different cues in a CRF framework to obtain an image's segmentation.

Hierarchical approaches. Many of the above approaches work well for data-driven smoothing, e.g., by edge-sensitive pairwise potentials, but are limited to rather local interaction. Long-range dependencies are difficult to model with a single-layered model and thus hierarchical graph structures are often employed to facilitate longer range dependencies with a tighter coupling of spatially distant variables.

Torralba et al. (2005) use boosted classifiers to model unary and interaction potentials in order to jointly label object and scene classes. Both are represented by a dictionary of patches. They use separate layers for each object and scene class and thus inference is costly due to the high graph connectivity. Results are presented on a single-scale database of static office scenes.

He et al. (2004) investigate a multi-scale approach for semantic scene labeling. They model the image on local, regional and global scale. On each scale different features are extracted to infer the hidden variables. In order to keep inference tractable no intra-layer pairwise interaction is modeled on the lowest layer. Thus, contextual knowledge can only be passed via the regional and global hidden variables. This work is extended by He et al. (2006) who add a-priori distributions over different contexts. For each context model, which is spatially defined for a super-pixel region, a separate CRF is employed and results are combined to obtain the final semantic segmentation.

A similar hierarchical model is proposed by Kumar and Hebert (2005). Their lowest layer consists of variables to model segmentation on the pixel or grid level. The second layer consists of a densely connected graph structure over object detections or super-pixels. Due to the dense connection on the second layer, inference in the joint model becomes prohibitive and therefore inference on both layers is interleaved. Results for this model are presented on three databases of static images. Single layer CRFs, as well as label smoothing MRFs with Potts potentials are significantly outperformed.

Verbeek and Triggs (2007) model the global context with a PLSA topic model. On the second layer a single additional node is inserted and connected to all variables on the lower level. This node models a topic distribution on class co-occurrence. However, this node does not impose any prior on the spatial distribution of these classes. This is left to the lower level's interaction potentials. This paper also proposes to learn the model's parameters from global topic annotations instead to learn them from fully pixel-wise labeled images, which are expensive to obtain. A similar model is adopted by Larlus et al. (2010) for object class segmentation. Here, the topic distribution models the appearance of a single object instance. Therefore, the additional topic node is only connected locally to hidden lower level variables of a segmentation blob.

Contrary to many others, Sudderth et al. (2008) do not classify images in a dense representation. They propose to segment a scene from keypoint detections with a scale estimate and build a hierarchical scene model in which they use Gibbs sampling for inference. The model for instance uses street as a reference point to constraint the position of cars. Thus, compared to pure appearance based recognition performance can improve. Their experiments show results for street scenes consisting of the classes road, street and car.

Kohli et al. (2009) propose a robust way to fuse multiple image segmentations. Potentials are defined over entire super-pixel regions in order to prevent over-smoothing from too simple pairwise potentials. As inference in such a highly connected model becomes computationally more and more demanding, a new variant of the graphcut algorithm is used for inference. Even though the impact by this model on the global accuracy is only minor, the results substantially improve visually as fine grained details are segmented much better. Ladicky et al. (2009) propose a generalization for this model and additionally allow interaction potentials on the super-pixel level. This model allows to exploit evidence on multiple levels and is thus similar to the one by Kumar and Hebert (2005). However, optimization is performed in one framework without interleaving inference on the individual layers.

Zhu et al. (2009) propose an hierarchical image parsing algorithm. Five layers model an image's semantic segmentation with a coarse to fine structure. Within each grid-structured layer the image grid cells are segmented into one out of 30 segmentation templates. Despite its simplicity and the sacrifice in accuracy by using templates for segmentation this approach yields competitive performance to state-of-the-art CRF models.

Onboard scene segmentation. Most of the above methods focus on static images of photo collections. However, most methods are not restricted to this domain and few works exist that employ similar techniques to handle scene segmentation for mobile platform onboard applications. Alon et al. (2006) propose a road segmentation approach to segment the drivable surface in desert terrain on single image frames. AdaBoost is employed on the Walsh-Hadamard filter bank responses to classify local image content into drivable or non-drivable.

Similarly to our extension of this work, Ess et al. (2009b) segment complete urban street sequences but additionally use stereo information. The semantically segmented scenes are used as intermediate representation to classify traffic situations. Temporal context is only modeled on the traffic situation level by using an Hidden Markov Model (HMM) to smooth the classification results. On the segmentation level only static image information is exploited and semantic context is leveraged from neighboring patches by an MRF framework.

Brostow et al. (2008) derive 3D features from structure from motion point clouds and employ them for semantic scene segmentation. Best performance is achieved when these features are additionally combined with appearance features in a randomized decision forest for classification. In particular under difficult lighting conditions, such as during dusk, this cue combination proves to be more robust than pure appearance based classification.

Sturgess et al. (2009) build on the same 3D features and a richer set of appearance features. A considerable performance improvement is achieved with graphcut inference in a hierarchical CRF framework (Ladicky et al., 2009). Similarly to the work by Brostow et al. (2008) motion and temporal information is only used to obtain the 3D point clouds. The CRF model that is employed for inferring the scene segmentation does not exploit temporal dynamics.

2.2.3 Relation to own work

Our work on semantic scene labeling in Chapter 6 is inspired by Alon et al. (2006) and Shotton et al. (2009). We extend the feature representation of Alon et al. (2006) by extracting filter banks on multiple scales. Moreover, we show that careful normalization with respect to lighting conditions by means of a gray world assumption allows to improve unary classification performance. Furthermore, our work aims at segmenting the entire scene and not only a single class.

While the employed CRF framework is inspired by Shotton et al. (2009) we improve their CRF formulation in various ways. Firstly, we introduce object nodes that are instantiated by a strong object class detector (Dalal and Triggs, 2005). These nodes allow a tight coupling of variables on the lattice layer by introducing a second layer of sparse nodes. While multiple layers have been used before – either in a dense fashion or with a graph structure deducted from super-pixels –, to the best of our knowledge, no previous work had leveraged an object class detector when we originally published our work. Our dynamic CRF model allows joint optimization and inference for both object and scene classes and provides an integrated approach for object detection and scene labeling. Note, that others (Gould et al., 2009b) have in the meanwhile also combined object detection with scene segmentation.

Moreover, our model allows multi-scale layout consistent modeling (Winn and Shotton, 2006) by exploiting the object detector's scale estimate. Also note, that our framework exploits the detector's confidence as additional unary potential for the second level object nodes.

Unlike most other models for semantic scene segmentation, we make use of temporal context by applying the notion of dynamic CRFs (McCallum et al., 2003). Even though dynamic CRFs have been used in the context of motion segmentation (e.g., Wang and Ji, 2005; Yin and Collins, 2007), none of the above models employs them for video scene understanding. It is important to note, that we use different dynamic models for objects and the background in highly dynamic scenes to cope with very different motion dynamics.

2.3 TRACKING

Unlike two-frame optic flow estimates or dynamic CRFs over few frames, classic multi-target tracking algorithms (Reid, 1979; Bar-Shalom and Fortmann, 1988; Rasmussen and Hager, 2001) typically aim to associate entities (e.g., multiple objects) over longer periods of time. As tracking is a large computer vision field on its own, we will review only related work on the most important aspects that are relevant for our work. In particular this is related literature on tracklets, MCMC methods for tracking and tracking-by-detection.

Tracking without detection. People tracking on visual data has been a goal in computer vision for several years. Even before the availability of strong object class detectors that allow tracking-by-detection, tracking approaches were investigated. These mostly rely on static cameras to perform background subtraction or color segmentation. Therefore, these methods are not amenable for deployment in mobile systems.

Popular methods include a tracker by Wren et al. (1997), who use a simple person model to track single persons in a low-dynamic environment by leveraging color information. Haritaoglu et al. (2000) track smaller groups of people in an outdoor surveillance environment. They use background subtraction as well as shape cues as image evidence. In a multi-people indoor surveillance setting Isard and MacCormick (2001) train a classifier based on low-level filter bank responses to densely segment the image in foreground and background. Their model employs a particle filter and is able to cope with inter-object occlusions by a 3D world model. Mittal and Davis (2003) track groups of people in a static multi-camera environment. They use stereo information to compute 3D positions and perform occlusion reasoning. Mean shift tracking proposed by Comaniciu et al. (2000) is at least in principle applicable to moving cameras. This approach tracks a blob's color distribution in real-time even under partial occlusion and can handle target articulation. One major common shortcoming of all these models is initialization that is performed manually or heuristically in many cases.

Tracking-by-Detection. With the availability of well performing and fast detection approaches (e.g., Viola and Jones, 2004) tracking-by-detection methods emerged. These approaches employ the detector's strong object model to obtain relatively reliable and robust per-frame image evidence. Many recent tracking approaches exploit this paradigm successfully.

Okuma et al. (2004) employ a boosted detector (Viola and Jones, 2004) in a particle filter tracking framework to track hockey players in TV broadcasts with moderately moving cameras. Detections are plugged into the sampling framework for the proposal distribution. This model is refined by Cai et al. (2006) with better occlusion handling. Moreover, the state is modeled in 3D by exploiting domain knowledge (i.e., the layout of a hockey rink), which supports more realistic dynamic models.

Wu and Nevatia (2007b) perform multi-pedestrian tracking in challenging surveillance videos. They employ their edgelet based detector (Wu and Nevatia, 2005), which individually detects several body parts. These are combined in a probabilistic tracking framework which is able to cope with partial occlusion. Missing detections are filled in by a mean shift tracker (Comaniciu *et al.*, 2000).

Breitenstein *et al.* (2009) track pedestrians with a Markovian particle filter framework and incorporate the detector's confidence directly into the observation model. Moreover, instance specific appearance models are learned for established tracks to facilitate data association. This approach generalizes to multiple detectors and results are shown for ISM (Leibe *et al.*, 2008a) and Dalal&Triggs detectors (Dalal and Triggs, 2005).

Online tracking-by-detection. While the above tracking-by-detection approaches detect object instances with a fixed appearance model, adaptive online learning methods also exist. Avidan (2007) proposes to use an online learning variant of AdaBoost in order obtain an instance specific detector. In each time frame the maximum detector response is used as a positive sample for a model update while the surrounding background windows are labeled as negative samples to obtain maximum separability.

Grabner and Bischof (2006) extend the online boosting approach by Oza (2001) with a more advanced feature selection strategy. Contrary to the approach by Avidan (2007) the weak learner's weights can be updated incrementally based on a single training sample with this approach. A further extension of this work (Grabner *et al.*, 2008) mitigates the drifting problem that often occurs for this group of algorithms by phrasing the tracking problem in a semi-supervised learning framework.

Babenko *et al.* (2009) address the drifting problem with online multi-instance boosting and show improved performance compared to the semi-supervised formulation. The advantage of the formulation as a multi-instance learning problem is that a bag of multiple potentially positive samples can be provided to update the tracker. On the contrary, the previously mentioned formulations rely on a single (potentially drifted) positive sample per update step.

Markov chain Monte Carlo tracking methods. Many traditional tracking methods employ Kalman filters (Kalman, 1960) which model the state's likelihood by means of Gaussian distributions. However, many real world problems are non-Gaussian and require more realistic distributions, which are often not amenable to analytic solutions. To remedy this shortcoming Markov chain Monte Carlo (MCMC) methods have been recently introduced in the domain of tracking. Instead of closed form solutions these methods sample the most likely state and provide a set of samples as approximation to the analytically intractable distributions.

Isard and Blake (1998) introduce particle filters to track the outline of shapes and find improved performance under severe background clutter compared to Kalman filters. Khan *et al.* (2005) apply Metropolis-Hastings MCMC to ant tracking with a variable number of objects. The interaction of multiple objects is modeled by an MRF prior. Their scenario is, however, limited to a static camera with uniform white background and well-defined entry and exit points. Moreover, ants only appear at a single fixed object scale.

Zhao *et al.* (2008) apply data-driven MCMC for efficient pedestrian tracking in 3D world coordinates with a Bayesian formulation. They use a static camera in a surveillance scenario and incorporate head detections as part of the proposal distribution to efficiently set up new objects. Their posterior, however, is independent of detection confidences but uses shape, background modeling and color cues in 2D image space. Song and Nevatia (2007) adapt this model for multi-view car tracking. In order to detect vehicles from all viewpoints the detector proposals are replaced by sampling the object center from a foreground probability map and the viewpoint from motion information.

Yu and Medioni (2009) aim to solve the association problem by sampling. Experiments show that their tracker handles occlusion and noisy evidence more gracefully than other approaches. Giebel et al. (2004) present a particle filter for pedestrian tracking from a moving vehicle in safety applications. Their model integrates shape, texture and stereo cues in the tracker's observation model. The shape cue in this work integrates a dynamic model for the human motion cycle based on "dynamic point distribution models" which are learned from training samples.

Lanz (2006) models multiple objects with individual particle filters for efficiency, but uses a joint dynamic model in order to cope with occlusion. Nummiaro et al. (2003) present a particle filter that is robust to partial occlusion and articulation. They track objects based on their color distribution and facilitate long-term tracking by adapting the color distribution over time when objects are tracked reliably.

Global optimal association. Leibe et al. (2008b) propose a coupled detection and tracking framework, which unlike many other methods does not rely on a Markovian assumption but aims at finding a globally optimal association of tracks to detections. They employ the maximum description length principle (MDL) for optimization and formulate a quadratic boolean optimization problem. This model does not handle individual tracks in isolation, but enforces that no two tracks occupy the same 3D point and that no image evidence is used twice.

Similar frameworks for global optimal tracking are proposed by Jiang et al. (2007), Berclaz et al. (2009) and Zhang et al. (2008), who formulate the optimization as linear programming problem or flow network optimization problem. Even though these tracking methods are designed for offline applications, they can be run in an online setting when optimization is performed in a sliding window.

Tracklets. Tracklets are an intermediate representation that group image evidence in neighboring image frames to ensure short-term consistency and to achieve a higher degree of robustness. Kaucic et al. (2005) track moving objects from a helicopter by bottom-up grouping detections to tracklets, which are linked to obtain longer tracks. This approach exploits a-priori scene knowledge to model expected occlusion regions. Tracklets that are spatially close to these occlusion maps but have a consistent motion and appearance signature are linked and therefore robustness with respect to occlusion is achieved. Perera et al. (2006) extend this work by introducing track splitting and merging to cope with spatially close objects that are often not easily separable from appearance.

A similar hierarchical tracking approach is presented by Huang et al. (2008), who track people in a surveillance scenario from a static camera. Further robustness in this work is achieved by estimating scene entry and exit points based on computed tracklets. Nillius *et al.* (2006) track soccer players with frequent object-object occlusion. They propose a tracking graph for linking individual tracks and propose a probabilistic formulation to resolve ambiguities in order to yield the most probable track configuration.

Yan *et al.* (2006) employ a tracklet strategy to track a tennis ball in low-resolution video. They grow tracklets from highly confident detections and link these with a graph-based approach. Andriluka *et al.* (2008) track humans through full occlusion in outdoor video sequences. Object parts are detected and linked with a hidden Markov model if they are consistent with the human walking cycle which is described by a low-dimensional hierarchical Gaussian process latent variable model. In case of occlusion the obtained tracklets are merged based on the individual tracklets' color appearance.

Li *et al.* (2009) exploit a discriminative boosting classifier to learn which tracklets should be linked in a hierarchical bottom-up tracking framework. This classifier learns track affinity based on 14 features including, e.g., track length, color and motion smoothness. Xing *et al.* (2009) track pedestrians with a two-stage particle filter framework in an online setting. Here, the extraction of local tracklets is coupled with a global process that manages longer term tracks. To achieve robustness only local tracklets that aggregate sufficient confidence are used to update the global tracks.

2.3.1 Relation to own work

Our work in Chapter 7 is related to the topic of tracking. It is inspired by recent tracking-by-detection methods as well as by the notion of tracklets. Contrary to existing work, we exploit the tracklet idea on the global scene level. Thus, we compute our scene observation model across multiple frames and ensure persistent detections, consistent semantic scene labels as well as a stable 3D geometry. To achieve robustness with a monocular setup we tightly integrate camera parameter estimation, tracking and 3D inference in a joint model. To compensate the camera's motion we rely on odometry information that is available in automotive and robotics applications from sensor readings.

For computational inference we employ data-driven MCMC sampling in a similar way as Khan *et al.* (2005) and Zhao *et al.* (2008). Contrary to both works, however, we perform online tracking from a moving platform in realistic urban and highway environments and therefore are not able to use background subtraction techniques or weak color segmentation to extract image evidence. We use a strong object class detector and semantic scene labels as single frame evidence.

Unlike Okuma *et al.* (2004) and Zhao *et al.* (2008) we do not only use object detections for the proposal distribution, but also exploit the confidence in our observation model. Contrary to most other works, we track multiple different object classes and exploit the object's class label for the dynamic model.

2.4 3D SCENE UNDERSTANDING

The final section of related work will focus on approaches to 3D scene understanding which encompasses to infer knowledge about the observed scene in a world coordinate frame. We briefly discuss approaches that infer low-level cues such as free space, scene depth or surface orientation, but focus on approaches that gain symbolic knowledge at a higher level. In particular, 3D object representations with a class label and 3D coordinates with respect to the camera are of interest to our work.

Free space and scene structure estimation. For navigation in robotic environments one crucial ability is to determine the free space, i.e., the 3D surface on that a vehicle can safely navigate. Labayrade et al. (2002) employ a stereo camera setup and extract a dense disparity map. Based on the disparity statistics piecewise linear surfaces are fitted to approximate the drivable ground by assuming that the majority of observed pixels belongs to the ground surface. Obstacles are found as outliers to the fitted planes in the disparity statistics.

Badino et al. (2007) propose to infer free space from stereo. Their approach exploits a occupancy grid representation and performs temporal integration over time. Additionally, they propose a dynamic programming algorithm that enforces spatial as well as temporal smoothness. Dahlkamp et al. (2006) aim to segment desert roads based on color for autonomous navigation in desert terrain. Their mixture of Gaussians color model is adaptively updated from samples that are located directly in front of the vehicle.

Contrary to the above methods, Nedevschi et al. (2004) do not explicitly segment the drivable surface but detect obstacles from sparse 3D stereo matches that are not on the ground level. Nedevschi et al. (2007) extend this approach to work with dense disparity maps. Breitenstein et al. (2008) use object detections to infer a scene's 3D structure and in particular its walkable surfaces. Webcam streams from static surveillance cameras are used as input. Walkability and depth are estimated from a dynamic Bayesian network, which incrementally updates parameters over time in an entropy minimization framework.

Depth and geometry estimation from monocular still images. While works discussed in the last paragraph frequently use stereo camera systems, we will now briefly discuss two approaches that infer scene properties from monocular still images. Hoiem et al. (2007a) segment images into super-pixels and classify them into ground, vertical regions and sky, while vertical regions are further classified with respect to their dominant surface orientation. Classification is based on a multi-feature approach, based on color, texture, location within the image and geometry features. When the segmentation results are fed into a sliding window object detector as additional context features these prove very discriminative for car detection.

Saxena et al. (2008) not only estimate surface orientation but aim to directly infer scene depth from low-level filter banks. Highly accurate training data is provided from a multi-sensor camera and laser scanner setup. To ensure global consistency and depth smoothness a hierarchical Markov random field model is applied as probabilistic model.

Scene understanding from still images. Understanding a scene's 3D layout from a single still image can easily be achieved by humans as we exploit several different cues. One of these cues is the relative depth of objects, which has successfully been used in computer vision recently. For computational reasoning an approximately flat ground plane is assumed. Additional constraints are that the camera is not subject to roll and is thus forward facing in the direction of the displayed objects. Thus, scene depth is a function of pitch and the image's y-coordinate.

Hoiem *et al.* (2008b) assume that objects stand on the ground plane. Therefore, the ground plane that is parametrized by the pitch (tilt) angle and known camera height is constrained by object detections and vice versa. By exploiting a Bayesian model they jointly infer the camera's pitch (which determines the ground plane) and the 3D position of objects. Besides object detections, surface orientation (Hoiem *et al.*, 2007a) is used as a further image cue. This work is extended and integrated with occlusion reasoning by Hoiem *et al.* (2008a) in an iterative framework. Various modules that estimate surface geometry, object-viewpoint relations and occlusion reasoning in separate models are run iteratively and successively refine and update the scene's model.

Gould *et al.* (2009a) propose a similar model and jointly infer ground plane, scene segmentation and surface geometry. This model, however, does not employ an object detector and uses a sampling technique for inference. Sampling is based on relabeling regions that are obtained from multiple differently parametrized image over-segmentations. Gould *et al.* (2009b) further improve this model and add an object detector driven term. Improved performance is found for pixel-wise scene labeling and object detection.

3D scene understanding from mobile platforms. Scene understanding from mobile platforms is one of the key ingredients for several applications including autonomous robots and vehicles as well as driver assistance for safety applications. In this paragraph we mostly focus on integrated systems with design principles that are at least in theory also applicable to other domains.

Early work on scene understanding in automotive driving was conducted by Betke *et al.* (2000) and Dickmanns (2007). Both works are motivated to develop a real-time system for autonomous driving in relatively uncluttered highway scenarios. To achieve this goal both systems exploit domain knowledge to drastically constrain the search space for objects and leverage temporal context to achieve robustness. For instance, they assume the existence of lane markings to define the boundary of the drivable surface. Moreover, the estimated lane is exploited to compute the horizon that is required to obtain depth by means of a ground plane assumption from monocular video. Both systems consist of rather independent modules like lane recognition and car detection. Due to the strong dependence on the availability of lane markings in these early systems, a failure to detect and track these will result in an overall system failure. Several problems of common lane tracking approaches are discussed in an evaluation by McCall and Trivedi (2006).

Grubb *et al.* (2004) present a 3D real-time system to detect pedestrians from a moving vehicle. They use a stereo camera and employ v-disparity as suggested by Labayrade *et al.* (2002) to detect obstacles. Segmented obstacles are classified with

2.4 3D SCENE UNDERSTANDING

frontal and side view pedestrian detectors (Papageorgiou and Poggio, 2000) and tracked with Kalman filters (Kalman, 1960) over time to achieve further robustness. This approach is evaluated on several sequences with varying difficulty, but only a single operation point is reported. Improved performance is found compared to a system with 2D image analysis only and to the system without tracking.

A similar approach is developed by Gavrila and Munder (2007). Their system employs a sparse stereo stage (Franke and Joos, 2000) to generate regions of interest. These are classified using a shape-based pedestrian detector (Gavrila and Philomin, 1999). For further robustness texture and depth cues are employed for an additional verification step. Tracking with independent Kalman filters ensures temporal consistency.

Gerónimo et al. (2010) build a system from similar independent modules. They use stereo to estimate ground plane parameters. Based on this estimate the regions of interest for potential pedestrians are defined by projecting a regular 3D grid with average pedestrian height to the image plane. The obtained set of windows is classified with a multi-cue classification approach, which uses Haar wavelets and HOG-like edge orientation histograms. Finally, positively classified regions are verified with a depth cue.

Bajracharya et al. (2009) propose a real-time robot system with a stereo camera for tracking pedestrians in urban and semi-urban environments. In their system the algorithm to generate regions of interest from the stereo depth map is a crucial component to achieve real-time. Identified regions are classified with shape-based features and tracked with a Kalman filter for temporal consistency. A visual odometry component is added for robustness with respect to odometry sensor failure. The achieved performance is among current state-of-the-art systems.

Cornelis et al. (2008) introduce the concept of cognitive loops to denote interacting modules. They integrate a real-time structure from motion approach and 3D facade reconstruction for urban environments with object recognition. Object recognition favors reconstruction as objects do not fulfill the underlying planar facade assumption. In turn city modeling facilitates object detection by providing a ground plane that is used to prune inconsistent detections such as detections suspended in the air.

Ess et al. (2009a) develop a state-of-the-art pedestrian detection and tracking system for urban environments that is most similar to our work. Unlike many other systems, which detect and track objects in isolation, this is one of the first systems that performs joint reasoning for multiple objects and the ground plane. It obtains object detections either from ISM (Leibe et al., 2008a), HOG (Dalal and Triggs, 2005) or the deformable part model by Felzenszwalb et al. (2009). If a sufficiently large fraction of the ground is visible, a stereo camera allows to estimate the camera's pose with respect to the ground plane from disparity. Single-frame joint inference is performed by belief propagation in a Bayesian network (Ess et al., 2007). A joint multi-object tracker (Leibe et al., 2008b) integrates results over time and a visual odometry module (Ess et al., 2008) is added to stabilize camera pose and ego-motion estimation with respect to the ground. While several modules in this system perform joint inference, they are rather loosely coupled by cognitive loops and failure of a single component may lead to a system failure. Hence, an additional failure recovery procedure is added to increase robustness. Gammeter *et al.* (2008) couple this system with human pose estimation (Jaeggli *et al.*, 2009).

2.4.1 Relation to own work

Chapter 7 presents a mobile system for joint high-level 3D inference from a monocular video and is thus related to the work discussed in this section. Contrary to most related work presented in this chapter (Gavrila and Munder, 2007; Grubb *et al.*, 2004; Bajracharya *et al.*, 2009; Ess *et al.*, 2009a), we rely only on a monocular camera and additionally estimate odometry information from sensor readings to compensate ego-motion. We emphasize that our model tightly integrates segmentation, detection, ground plane estimation and tracking and enables joint inference with reversible jump MCMC. Objects constrain the ground plane and vice versa. Consistency with semantic scene labeling and tracklet continuity over time allows to substantially increase our system's robustness. To the best of our knowledge none of the above systems is known to work under these constraints. Out of the above systems, only Gould *et al.* (2009a) and Gould *et al.* (2009b) use semantic scene labels to improve 3D scene understanding. Their model, however, relies on computationally more demanding super-pixel representations and is designed for still images.

Furthermore, we not only show results for a single object class, but for three object classes and also we include a multi-class dataset. One of the datasets for our experiments is recorded in a dense urban environment and direct comparison to the most similar work by Ess *et al.* (2009a) shows that our system yields state-of-the-art detection performance with a single camera. We also consistently outperform object tracking with independent Kalman filters, which is adopted in many of the referred works above.

EVALUATION OF STATIC FEATURES FOR PEOPLE DETECTION 3

Contents

3.1	Introduction	**42**
3.2	Features and classifiers	**42**
	3.2.1 Features	43
	3.2.2 Classifiers	45
3.3	Dataset and methodology	**45**
3.4	Evaluation criterion	**46**
3.5	Experiments	**47**
	3.5.1 Single feature detection	47
	3.5.2 Multi-cue detection	48
	3.5.3 Failure analysis	52
3.6	Conclusion	**53**

In this chapter, we provide a thorough and systematic evaluation of sliding window detectors for the task of people detection in static images. Compared to keypoint-based detection schemes (e.g., ISM, Leibe et al., 2008a) the sliding window framework is more suitable for detection from onboard platforms for two reasons. Firstly, for many onboard applications the resolution of the available image stream is rather limited and keypoint detectors tend to work less robustly on small scales. And secondly, keypoint based methods often rely on an unreliable scale estimate to perform multi-scale detection, whereas sliding window approaches typically scan all scales exhaustively, which is often more robust.

Additionally, we propose a new descriptor which is based on the dense sampling of shape context (Belongie et al., 2002). As a testbed we use the well known *INRIA Person* database (Dalal and Triggs, 2005). Contrary to previous work (see Chapter 2), we do not only show performance with a specific combination of feature and classifier but exhaustively evaluate several combinations of features and classifiers. Furthermore, we refrain from the common evaluation in terms of false positives per window (FPPW) but rather use full image based evaluation metrics.

Experimentally, we show that full image based metrics, such as precision and recall or false positives per image, provide a better measure for the detector's performance (see Section 3.4 for a discussion and Dollár et al. (2009b) for more details). Additionally, our experiments indicate that the combination of complementary features allows to improve detector performance. We conclude this chapter with an analysis of the most prominent failure cases.

3.1 INTRODUCTION

People are one of the most challenging classes for object detection, mainly due to large variations caused by articulation and appearance. Recently, several researchers have reported impressive results (Papageorgiou and Poggio, 2000; Dalal and Triggs, 2005; Seemann et al., 2006) for this task. Broadly speaking there are two types of approaches. Sliding window methods exhaustively scan the input images over position and scale independently classifying each sliding window (e.g., Papageorgiou and Poggio, 2000; Viola and Jones, 2004; Dalal and Triggs, 2005), while other methods generate hypotheses by evidence aggregation (e.g., Seemann et al., 2006; Forsyth and Fleck, 1997; Wu and Nevatia, 2005; Felzenszwalb and Huttenlocher, 2000; Mikolajczyk et al., 2004). To the best of our knowledge at the time when we first conducted this study only two comparative studies on people detection methods existed. Seemann et al. (2005) compare local features and interest point detectors while Munder and Gavrila (2006) compare various sliding window detectors. However, Munder and Gavrila (2006) are focused on automotive applications and their database only consists of cropped gray scale image windows. In the meanwhile, several other authors got interested in detailed performance evaluations of pedestrian detectors. Enzweiler and Gavrila (2009) evaluate several detectors in an automotive system, while we extended our work with Dollár et al. (2009b) by introducing a new benchmark with a detailed state-of-the-art evaluation.

While the evaluation on single image windows is interesting for the classifier's design, it does not allow to assess the detection performance in real-world scenes where many false positive detections may arise from body parts or at wrong scales. This chapter therefore contributes a systematic evaluation of various features and classifiers proposed for sliding window approaches where we assess the performance of the different components and the overall detectors on entire real-world images rather than on cropped image windows.

This chapter contributes a systematic evaluation of different feature representations for general people detection in combination with discriminant classifiers on full size images. We also introduce a new feature based on dense sampling of the Shape Context (Belongie et al., 2002). Additionally, several feature combination schemes are evaluated and show an improvement over state-of-the-art (Dalal and Triggs, 2005) people detection.

This chapter is structured as follows. Section 3.2 reviews the evaluated features and classifiers. Section 3.3 introduces the experimental protocol, Section 3.4 discuses evaluation criteria and Section 3.5.1 gives results for single cue detection. Results for cue combination are discussed in Section 3.5.2 and Section 3.5.3 analyzes failure cases. Section 3.6 will summarize our work and draw conclusions.

3.2 FEATURES AND CLASSIFIERS

Sliding window object detection systems for static images usually consist of two major components which we evaluate separately in this work. The *feature* component encodes the visual appearance of the object to be detected, whereas the *classifier* determines for

3.2 FEATURES AND CLASSIFIERS 43

	Linear SVM	Kernel SVM	Ada-Boost	Other	Criterion
Haar wavelet (Papageorgiou and Poggio, 2000)		polynomial			ROC
Haar-like wavelet (Viola and Jones, 2004)			cascaded		ROC
Histograms of orient gradients (Dalal and Triggs, 2005)	✓	RBF			FPPW
Shapelets (Sabzmeydani and Mori, 2007)			✓		FPPW
Shape Context (Seemann et al., 2005)				ISM	RPC

Table 3.1: Original combination of features and classifiers

each sliding window independently whether it contains the object or not.

Table 3.1 gives an overview of the feature/classifier combinations proposed in the literature. As can be seen from this table, many possible feature/classifier combinations are left unexplored therefore making it difficult to assess the respective contribution of different features and classifiers to the overall detector performance. To enable a comprehensive evaluation using all possible feature/classifier combinations, we reimplemented the respective methods. Comparisons with published binaries (whenever available) verifies that our re-implementations perform at least as good as the originally proposed feature/classifier combinations (cf. Figure 3.1). The remainder of this section reviews the evaluated features and classifiers.

3.2.1 Features

Haar wavelets have first been proposed by Papageorgiou and Poggio (2000) for people detection. They introduce a dense over-complete representation using wavelets at the scale of 16 and 32 pixel with an overlap of 75%. Three different types are used, which allow to encode low frequency changes in contrast: vertical, horizontal and diagonal. Thus, the overall length of the feature vector for a 64 × 128 pixel detection window is 1326 dimensions. In order to cope with lighting differences, for each color channel only the maximum response is kept and normalization is performed according to the window's mean response for each direction. Additionally, the original authors report that for the class of people the wavelet coefficient's sign is not carrying information due to the variety in clothing. Hence, only the absolute values for each coefficient is kept. During our experiments we found that an additional L_2 length normalization with regularization of the feature vector improves performance.

Haar-like features have been proposed by Viola and Jones (2004) as a generalization of Haar wavelets with arbitrary dimensions and different orientations (efficiently computed by integral images). They suggest to exhaustively use all possible features that

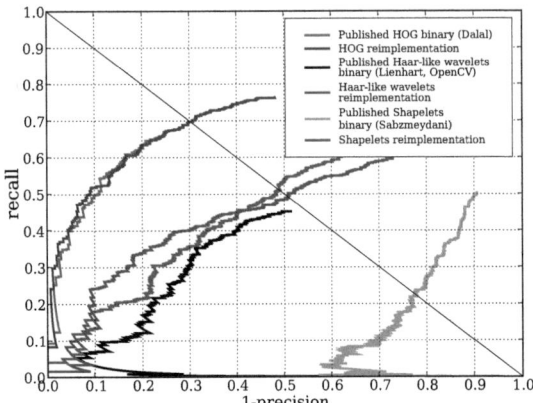

Figure 3.1: Performance of available detector binaries and our implementations; for Haar-like wavelets we improved regularization, for Shapelets we set the regularization properly

can be sampled from a sliding window and let AdaBoost select the most discriminative ones. Thus, their approach is computationally limited to rather small detection window sizes. For our evaluation we use the OpenCV[3] implementation of their algorithm to select the relevant features and only use those appropriately scaled to our detection window's size of 64×128 pixels. Similarly to Papageorgiou and Poggio (2000) we found that for the class of people the coefficient's sign is irrelevant due to different clothing and surroundings and therefore used absolute values. Moreover, we found that the applied illumination variance normalization performs worse than simple L_2 length normalization on the selected features.

Histograms of oriented gradients (HOG) have been proposed by Dalal and Triggs (2005). Image derivatives are computed by centered differences in x- and y-direction. The gradient magnitude is then inserted into cell histograms (8×8 pixels), interpolating in x, y and orientation. Blocks are groups of 2×2 cells with an overlap of one cell in each direction. Blocks are L_2 length normalized with an additional hysteresis step to avoid one gradient entry to dominate the feature vector. The final vector is constituted of all normalized block histograms with a total dimension of 3780 for a 64×128 detection window.

Shapelets (Sabzmeydani and Mori, 2007) are another type of gradient-based feature obtained by selecting salient gradient information. They employ discrete AdaBoost on densely sampled gradient image patches of multiple orientations ($0°, 90°, 180°, 270°$) at the scales of 5 to 15 pixels to classify those locally into people and non-people based

---

[3] http://sourceforge.net/projects/opencvlibrary

on the local shape of the object. As preprocessing step, gradient images are smoothed to account for inaccuracies of the person's position within the annotation. Moreover, the underlying gradient image is normalized shapelet-wise to achieve illumination invariance. Compared to the published source code[4] we use stronger regularization for the normalization step, in order not to amplify noise. This improves the results considerably as shown in Figure 3.1.

Shape Context has originally been proposed as a feature point descriptor (Belongie et al., 2002) and has shown excellent results for people detection in the generative ISM framework (Leibe et al., 2005; Seemann et al., 2006). The descriptor is based on edges which are extracted with a Canny detector (Canny, 1986). Those are stored in a log-polar histogram with location being quantized in nine bins. For the radius 9, 16 and 23 pixels are used, while orientation is quantized into four bins. For sliding window search we densely sampled the feature on a regular lattice with a support of 32 pixels (other scales in the range from 16 to 48 pixels performed worse). For our implementation we used the version of Mikolajczyk and Schmid (2005) which additionally applies PCA to reduce the feature dimensionality to 36 dimensions. The overall length of all descriptors concatenated for one test window is 3024.

3.2.2 Classifiers

The second major component for sliding window approaches is the deployed classifier. For the classification of single windows two popular choices are SVMs and the AdaBoost framework in conjunction with decision tree stumps. SVMs optimize a hyperplane to separate positive and negative training samples based on the *global* feature vector. Different kernels map the classification problem to a higher dimensional feature space. For our experiments we used the implementation *SVM Light* (Joachims, 1999). In contrast, boosting is picking *single entries* of the feature vector with the highest discriminative power in order to minimize the classification error in each round.

3.3 DATASET AND METHODOLOGY

To evaluate the performance for the introduced features and their combination with different classifiers we use the established INRIA Person dataset[5]. This dataset contains images of humans taken from several viewpoints under varying lighting conditions in indoor and outdoor scenes. For training and testing the dataset is split into three subsets: the full size positive images, the scale-normalized crops of humans and full size negative images. Table 3.2 gives an overview of the number of images and the number of overall depicted people.

For training we use all 2416 positive images and for the negative training instances we randomly cropped a fixed set of 10 negative windows from every negative image.

---
[4]formerly http://www.cs.sfu.ca/~mori/research/shapelet_detect
[5]http://pascal.inrialpes.fr/data/human

	Positive set/ # instances	Normalized crops set	Negative set
Training	615 / 1208	2416	1218
Testing	288 / 566	1132	453

Table 3.2: Number of images and instances for the INRIA Person dataset

Unlike the original authors (Dalal and Triggs, 2005) we test the trained detectors on the full images. We do so, in order not only to evaluate the detector in terms of false positive detections per window (FPPW), but with respect to their frequency and spatial distribution. This gives a more realistic assessment on how well a detector performs for real image statistics (cf. discussion in Section 3.4). To allow this evaluation in terms of recall and precision, the nearby initial detections in scale and space need to be merged to a single final hypothesis. To achieve this, a mode seeking adaptive-bandwidth mean shift algorithm (Comaniciu, 2003) is used. The width of the smoothing kernel was kept fixed for all experiments and no further post-processing was applied. Ground truth and final detections are matched using the PASCAL criterion (Everingham et al., 2010), which demands a minimum overlap of 50% to match a ground truth annotation with a detection.

3.4 EVALUATION CRITERION

Before we present our results, we briefly discuss the disadvantages of frequently used (see Table 3.1) FPPW and ROC metrics. Window based evaluation protocols consider missed recall versus the number of false positives per window or detection rate versus false positive rate respectively. Scores for positive windows are obtained by classifying single cropped windows containing a pedestrian, while scores for negative windows are collected by exhaustively scanning a different negative set. Most recent works compare their performance on the popular INRIA Person database in terms of false positives per windows (FPPW); even though window based measures are subject to the following severe drawbacks:

- Since the negative sets usually do not contain any pedestrians, false positives arising from detections on body parts or at a wrong scale will never appear and will be disregarded.
- As the negative set in some cases (e.g., Dalal and Triggs, 2005) is chosen to be from several different domains, the obtained statistics on false detections does not necessarily indicate the performance in real application environments.
- The density of scanning on the negative set is important and needs to be obeyed for comparable results. Scanning the negative images with a lower resolution might lead to fewer false positive detections and thus to a virtual better performance.
- A comparison with non-window based detection systems (e.g., Leibe et al., 2008a; Lampert et al., 2009; Stark et al., 2009) is impossible by design of the window

3.5 EXPERIMENTS

based evaluation scheme.
- Depending on the detector, non-maximum suppression methods have the potential to further decrease the number of false detections. Window based metrics only evaluate the score of single windows in isolation and do not assess, the possibly complex, interaction with nearby windows.
- Boundary artifacts for the cropped positive samples might lead to unique features on which a learned classifier can overfit. Such a classifier will not be able to generalize well on full sized images. Window based evaluations can not detect this kind of problem. In the recent past few papers (e.g., Sabzmeydani and Mori, 2007; Maji et al., 2008) have suffered from this issue and over-reported performance.

Thus, we believe that image based measures such as Recall-Precision curves or False Positive Per Image (FPPI) plots, which have none of the above shortcomings, should be preferred to obtain a better assessment. For an experimental comparison of window based and image based metrics we refer to Dollár et al. (2009b). In this work we show that the order of algorithm performance changes substantially when image based measures are employed to evaluate detectors in a full detector setup compared to the isolated classifier evaluation by FPPW.

3.5 EXPERIMENTS

3.5.1 Single feature detection

We start by evaluating all features individually in combination with the three classifiers AdaBoost, linear SVM and RBF kernel SVM. In order not to introduce a bias by the selection of negative samples a fixed set was used and no bootstrap learning was employed. Figures 3.2 shows the results we have obtained.

First of all, the HOG descriptor and the similar Shape Context descriptor consistently outperform the other features independent of the learning algorithm. They are able to achieve around 60% equal error rate. The two Haar-like wavelet-based approaches perform similar, while the Haar features by Papageorgiou and Poggio (2000) perform slightly better in combination with AdaBoost and the Haar-like features by Viola and Jones (2004) show better results when combined with a linear SVM. Shapelets are not performing as well as suggested by the reported FPPWs in the original paper. Only in combination with a linear SVM they do better than the wavelet features.

Overall, RBF kernel SVMs together with the gradient-based features HOG and Shape Context show the best results. All features except shapelets show better performance with the RBF kernel SVM compared to the linear SVM. AdaBoost achieves a similarly good performance in comparison with RBF kernel SVMs in particular for the Haar-like wavelet, the HOG feature and for shapelets. It does slightly worse for the dense Shape Context descriptor. For the wavelet features, linear SVMs are not able to learn a good classifier with limited data. AdaBoost and RBF kernel SVMs are doing better in this case due to their ability to separate data non-linearly. Remarkably, linear SVMs show better performance in combination with Shape Context compared to HOG. This might

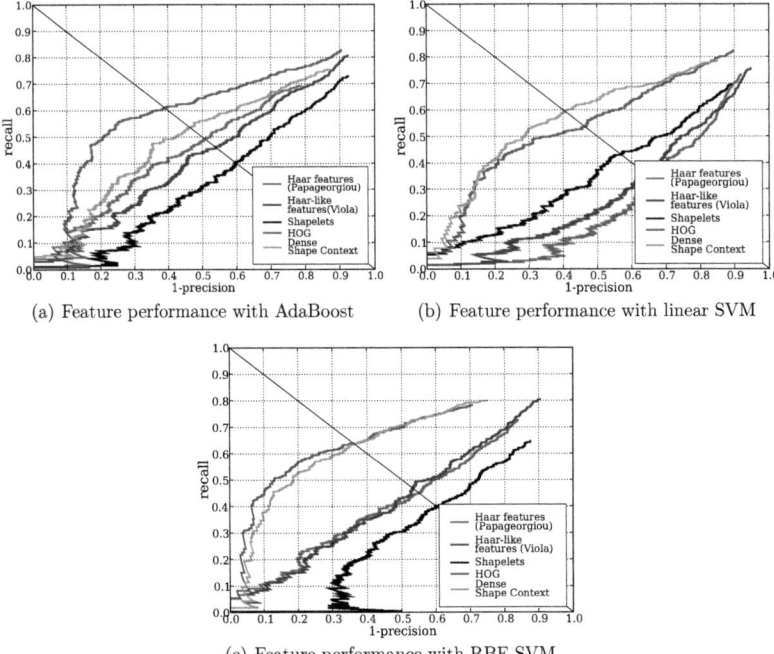

Figure 3.2: Recall-Precision detector performances with single features

be an effect of the log-polar sampling for the feature histograms which allows for a better linear separation.

3.5.2 Multi-cue detection

A closer look on the single detectors' complementarity reveals that different features in combination with different classifiers do perform differently on the individual instances. This can be explained by the fact that the features encode different information. While gradients encode high frequency changes in the images, Haar wavelets as they are proposed by Papageorgiou and Poggio (2000) also encode much lower frequencies. Thus, it is worth to further investigate the combination of features. To this end, we conducted several experiments employing early integration with linear SVMs and AdaBoost as classifier. RBF kernel SVMs have not further been employed for computational complexity reasons.

Before stacking feature vectors in a linear SVM classifier, each feature cue was L_2 length normalized to avoid a bias resulting from the features' scale range. In order to

3.5 EXPERIMENTS

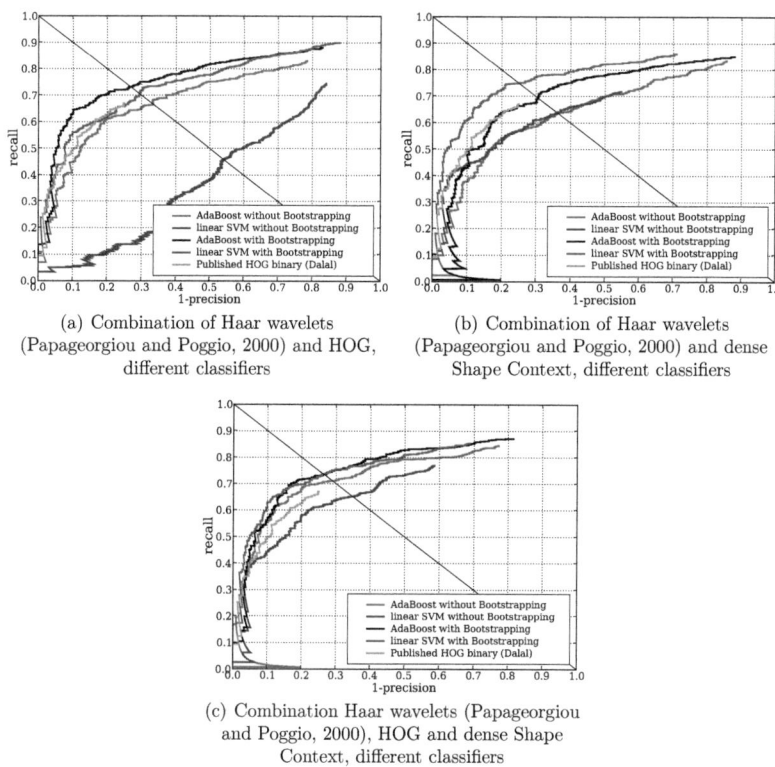

Figure 3.3: Recall-Precision detector performances with multiple features

keep the comparison fair, we also used the same normalization for AdaBoost. We have combined all possible subsets of HOG, Shape Context and Haar wavelet-based features (Papageorgiou and Poggio, 2000). Combinations with shapelets have not been tried due to the poor performance of the feature itself. In the following we will focus on the combinations which yielded the best results.

Additionally we also employed a bootstrapping method, which has shown to improve performance (Dalal and Triggs, 2005; Munder and Gavrila, 2006). For this an initial classifier is trained with all available positive training data and random negative samples. Then "hard examples" are collected by scanning the negative training images. The final classifier is then trained on the set of the initial and hard samples.

Our most successful experiments yielded results as depicted in Figure 3.3. For easier comparison the curve of the best performing published[6] binary (Dalal and Triggs, 2005,

---

[6] http://pascal.inrialpes.fr/soft/olt

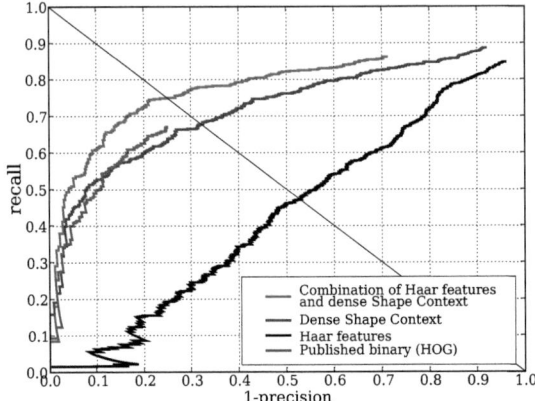

Figure 3.4: Bootstrapped single feature detectors of Figure 3.4(b) and their combination, linear SVM

bootstrapped SVM classifier) is also shown. Figure 3.4(a) shows the performance of Haar wavelets (Papageorgiou and Poggio, 2000) and HOG features. Even without bootstrapping, the combined features with the AdaBoost classifier almost reach the performance of the published HOG binary. This is due to local optimization of AdaBoost that concentrates on the most discriminative feature in each round. An analysis shows that 67.5% are HOG features while 32.5% are Haar features. The performance of SVM with this feature combination is in between the performance of the two original features. This result can be explained by the global optimization strategy of SVMs, which needs more data to obtain a good fit. Obviously, the bootstrapping method provides more data and consequently performance increases substantially to little above the performance of the bootstrapped HOG features. However, it does not reach the performance of the bootstrapped AdaBoost classifier. As already discussed in Section 3.5.1, AdaBoost is doing better in separating HOG features and Haar wavelets when used individually. Thus, it is only little surprising for the combination to perform also well.

Figure 3.4(b) shows the combination of dense Shape Context features with Haar wavelets. Without bootstrapping AdaBoost and linear SVM perform similar and better than for the single features alone. Adding bootstrapping the SVM classifier again gains a significant improvement. This is due to the same fact we have pointed out in Section 3.5.1. Shape Context features show good linear separability and thus linear SVMs are able to achieve a high classification performance. Again we reviewed the features chosen by AdaBoost. Those were 66.25% Shape Context features and 33.75% Haar wavelet features. We also analyzed the performance of the individual features in a linear SVM when learned with a bootstrapping strategy. Figure 3.4 shows, that in fact both features on their own cannot reach the performance that is reached with their combination. Compared to the state-of-the-art HOG object detector we improve recall

3.5 EXPERIMENTS

Figure 3.5: Sample detections at a precision of 80%; Red bounding boxes denote false detections, while yellow bounding boxes denote true positives. First row shows detection by the publicly available HOG detector (Dalal and Triggs, 2005); second row depicts sample detections for our combination of dense Shape Context with Haar wavelets in a linear SVM

considerably about 10% at 80% precision.

Finally, Figure 3.4(c) shows results of the combination of HOG, Shape Context and Haar features. For this combination AdaBoost already outperforms the HOG object detector by Dalal and Triggs (2005) even without bootstrapping. The linear SVM classifier again profits from the bootstrapping step and performs similarly to the bootstrapped AdaBoost classifier. Interestingly, the performance obtained by the combination of HOG, Shape Context and Haar features is highly similar to the pairwise combinations of Haar features with either HOG or Shape Context. Here the analysis on the chosen features yields the following distribution: 45.25% HOG, 34.0% Shape Context, 20.75% Haar. Additionally adding Haar-like features (Viola and Jones, 2004) resulted in almost unchanged detections.

In summary we can state that the combination of different features is successful to improve state-of-the-art people detection performance. We have shown, that a combination of HOG features and Haar wavelets in a AdaBoost classification framework as well as dense Shape Context features with Haar wavelets in a linear SVM framework are able to achieve about 10% better recall with a precision of 80% compared to a single feature HOG detector. Figure 3.5 shows the improvement on sample images. Similarly to Levi and Weiss (2004) we also observe that a combination of features can achieve better detection performance than the standalone features when trained on the same amount of training data. Additionally, SVMs were able to benefit from a bootstrapping strategy during learning as noted by Munder and Gavrila (2006). While AdaBoost also improves by bootstrapping, the effect is much weaker compared to SVMs.

52 CHAPTER 3. EVALUATION OF STATIC FEATURES FOR PEOPLE DETECTION

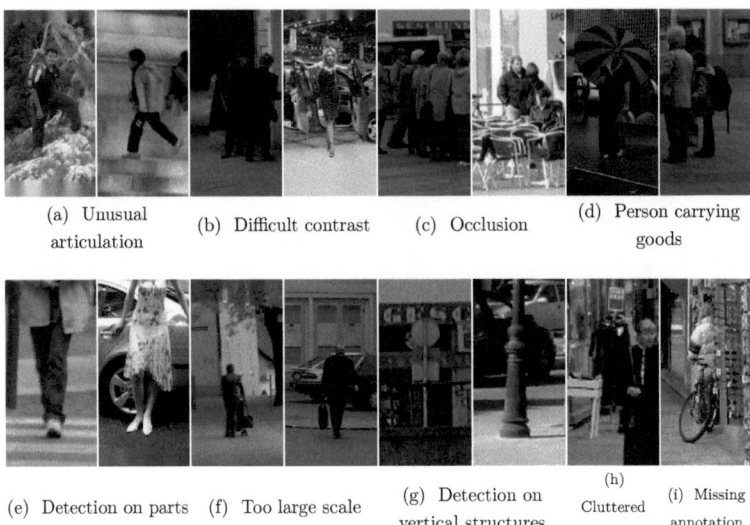

(a) Unusual articulation (b) Difficult contrast (c) Occlusion (d) Person carrying goods

(e) Detection on parts (f) Too large scale (g) Detection on vertical structures (h) Cluttered background (i) Missing annotation

Figure 3.6: Missed recall (upper row) and false positive detections (lower row) at equal error rate

3.5.3 Failure analysis

To complete our experimental evaluation we also conducted a failure case analysis. In particular, we have analyzed the missing recall and the false positive detections at equal error rate (149 missing detections/ 149 false positives) for the feature combination of Shape Context and Haar wavelets in combination with a linear SVM. Missing recall mainly occurred due to unusual articulations (37 cases), difficult background or contrast (44 cases), occlusion or carried bags (43 cases), under- or overexposure (18 cases) and due to detection at too large or too small scales (7). There were also 3 cases which were detected with the correct height but could not be matched to the annotation according to the PASCAL criterion due to the very narrow annotation.

False positive detections can be categorized as follows: Vertical structures like poles or street signs (54 cases), cluttered background (31 cases), too large scale detections with people in lower part (24 cases), too low scale on body parts (28 cases). There were also a couple of "false" detections (12 cases) on people which were not annotated in the database (mostly due to occlusion or at small scales). Some samples of missed people and false positives are shown in Figure 3.6.

3.6 CONCLUSION

In this chapter we have presented a systematic performance evaluation of state-of-the-art features and classification algorithms for people detection. Experiments on the challenging INRIA Person dataset showed that both HOG and dense Shape Context perform better than other features independent of the deployed classifier. Moreover, we have shown that a combination of multiple features is able to improve the performance of the individual detectors considerably. Clearly, there are several open issues which cannot be solved easily with single image classification. Thus, additional motion features (see Chapter 4) and the integration across multiple frames are necessary to further improve performance (see Chapter 7). Motion for instance can help to resolve false detections due to vertical structures while multiple frame integration is likely to yield better results with cluttered background.

4 MULTI-CUE ONBOARD PEDESTRIAN DETECTION

Contents

4.1	Introduction	**55**
4.2	Features and classifiers	**58**
	4.2.1 Features	58
	4.2.2 Classifiers	59
4.3	Learning and testing	**60**
	4.3.1 Improved learning procedure	60
	4.3.2 Testing	61
4.4	New dataset	**62**
4.5	Results	**63**
4.6	Conclusion	**69**

THIS chapter extends our work on people detection of the previous chapter by improving on the deployed features, the classifiers and on several important implementation details. In particular, it builds on the results obtained for static features in Chapter 3 and enriches our object description with features derived from motion in image pairs.

Moreover, we focus on the detection of pedestrians in this chapter. This scenario is more challenging as pedestrians appear at small scales and are seen from the full range of viewpoints. Additionally, camera motion complicates the use of motion information. Due to non-static background, background substraction techniques as frequently used in the surveillance domain (e.g., Stauffer and Grimson, 2000; Elgammal et al., 2000; Sharma and Davis, 2007; Ko et al., 2008) are not an option.

To evaluate our work, we introduce a new dataset which is recorded from a moving car (see Figure 4.1) under real-world conditions in an urban environment. Additionally, we compare our work on three datasets from previous literature (Ess et al., 2007). Our experimental results show that motion features consistently improve detection performance on all four datasets.

4.1 INTRODUCTION

Detecting pedestrians using an onboard camera is a challenging problem but an important component, e.g., for robotics and automotive safety applications. While psychologists and neuroscientists argue that motion is an important cue for human perception (Gibson, 1979) only few computer vision object detectors (e.g., Viola et al., 2005; Dalal et al., 2006) exploit this fact. Interestingly, Viola et al. (2005) showed improved detection performance but for static cameras only. It is unclear how to transfer their results to onboard sequences. In contrast, Dalal *et al.* (2006) proposed motion features that are – at least in principle – applicable to onboard sequences. While Dalal *et al.* (2006) showed improved performance using the FPPW evaluation criterion (false positives per window) they were unable to outperform their own static HOG feature (Dalal and Triggs, 2005) in a complete detector setting (Dalal, 2006).

The second avenue we follow in this chapter is to incorporate multiple and complementary features for detection. While Varma and Ray (2007) convincingly showed that multiple features improve performance for image classification, for detection only few approaches exploit this fact (Wu and Nevatia, 2008; Gavrila, 2007; Wojek and Schiele, 2008b).

The third avenue of this chapter is related to the classifier choice. Popular classifiers are SVMs (Shashua *et al.*, 2004; Dalal and Triggs, 2005; Felzenszwalb *et al.*, 2008; Maji *et al.*, 2008; Lin and Davis, 2008) or boosting (Viola and Jones, 2004; Dollár *et al.*, 2008; Wu and Nevatia, 2007a; Sabzmeydani and Mori, 2007). However, the large intra-class variability of pedestrians seems to require a more careful design of the classifier framework. Several authors have argued that, e.g., viewpoint variation requires a different classifier design. Wu and Nevatia (2007a) remedy this issue by learning a tree structured classifier, Lin and Davis (2008) use a handcrafted hierarchy, while Seemann *et al.* (2006) propose multi-articulation learning. Gavrila (2007) proposes a tree-structured Bayesian approach that builds on offline clustering of pedestrian shapes. What is common to these approaches is that they treat the problem of data partitioning and classifier learning separately. In this chapter however we address this problem in a more principled way by using the MPLBoost classifier (Babenko *et al.*, 2008) that simultaneously learns the data partitions and a strong classifier for each partition. Multiple strong AdaBoost classifiers are learned jointly in this framework each one focusing on a subpart of the data. Moreover, clusters of similar data are determined automatically based on discriminative features and thus no preprocessing such as clustering is required.

The main focus of this chapter is to advance the state-of-the-art in pedestrian detection for realistic and challenging onboard datasets. For this we experimentally evaluate combinations of features and classifiers and address the problem of learning a multi-viewpoint pedestrian detector.

Our contribution is threefold. Firstly, we show that motion cues provide a valuable feature, also for detection from a moving platform. Secondly, we show that MPLBoost and histogram intersection kernel SVMs can successfully learn a multi-viewpoint pedestrian detector and often outperform linear SVMs. Thirdly, a new realistic and publicly available onboard dataset (*TUD-Brussels*) containing multi-viewpoint data is introduced. It is accompanied by one of the first training datasets (*TUD-MotionPairs*) containing image pairs which allow to extract and train from motion features. These two datasets will enable comparison of different approaches based on motion. Besides these contributions we discuss several important algorithmic details that prove important and that are often neglected and overlooked.

This chapter is structured as follows. Section 4.2 introduces features and classifiers

4.1 INTRODUCTION

Figure 4.1: Row 1 and 3 show detections obtained with our detector in an urban environment. Row 2 and 4 show the according flow fields (Zach et al., 2007); note the detector's robustness to camera motion even when ego-motion dominates the optic flow field. For the optic flow color coding see Figure 4.4(b).

and Section 4.3 discusses several important technical details. Section 4.4 introduces datasets while Section 4.5 discusses the experimental results and Section 4.6 concludes.

4.2 FEATURES AND CLASSIFIERS

In the following subsections we will discuss the features (Section 4.2.1) and classifiers (Section 4.2.2) which we deploy in a sliding window framework.

4.2.1 Features

A wide range of features has been proposed for pedestrian detection. Here, we focus on three successful features containing complementary information (see Chapter 3 for a wider range of static image features). While HOG features encode high frequency gradient information, Haar wavelets encode lower frequency changes in the color channels. Oriented Histograms of Flow features exploit optical flow and thus a complementary cue.

HOG. Histograms of oriented gradients have originally been proposed by Dalal and Triggs (2005). The bounding box is divided into 8×8 pixel *cells* containing histograms of oriented gradients. 2×2 cells constitute a *block* which is the neighborhood to perform normalization. For people detection L_2-norm with an additional hysteresis performs best.

Haar. Haar wavelets have been introduced by Papageorgiou and Poggio (2000) for people detection. Those provide an overcomplete representation using features at the scale of 32 and 16 pixels. Similarly to HOG blocks, wavelets overlap by 75%. As proposed we use the absolute responses of horizontal, vertical and diagonal wavelet types.

Oriented histograms of flow. The motion feature we use throughout this chapter is the Internal Motion Histogram wavelet difference (IMHwd) descriptor described by Dalal *et al.* (2006). The descriptor combines 9 bins per histogram on 8×8 pixel cells, with interpolation only for histogram bins. It is computed by applying wavelet-like operators on a 3×3 cell grid, letting pixel-wise differences of flow vectors vote into histogram bins. We use IMHwd due to its consistently better performance in previous experiments compared to other proposed descriptors. The flow field is computed using the TV-L_1 algorithm by Zach *et al.* (2007), which provides regularization while allowing for discontinuities in the flow field. Contrary to Dalal *et al.* (2006), we compute the optical flow for the training samples on full images instead of crops, which is particularly important for the regularized TV-L_1 flow. We also conducted experiments with the unregularized flow algorithm described in Dalal *et al.* (2006), but it resulted in a slight loss of performance compared to the algorithm by Zach *et al.* (2007) (cf. Figure 4.3(a)). For further discussion see Section 4.5.

4.2 FEATURES AND CLASSIFIERS

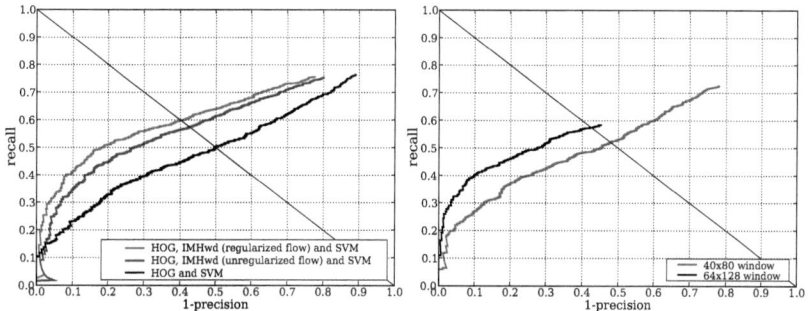

(a) Performance for different flow algorithms – using the regularized flow algorithm by Zach et al. (2007) works best

(b) Performance drops when using a smaller detection window.

Figure 4.2: Impact of flow algorithm and detection window size

Feature combination. In the experiments reported below we analyze various combinations of the above features. To combine features we L_2-normalize each cue-component and concatenate all subvectors. The concatenated feature vector is then fed into the classifier algorithm.

4.2.2 Classifiers

The second major component for sliding window based detection systems is the employed classifier. Most popular choices are linear SVMs and AdaBoost. As discussed before these are not perfectly suited because of the high intra-class variability of humans, e.g., caused by multiple viewpoints and appearance differences. In this chapter we therefore explore the applicability of MPLBoost that learns data clusters and strong classifiers for these clusters simultaneously.

SVM. Linear SVMs learn the hyperplane that optimally separates pedestrians from background in a high-dimensional feature space. Extensions to kernel SVMs are possible, allowing to transfer the data to a higher and potentially infinitely dimensional representation as for RBF kernels. For detection however, kernel SVMs are rarely used due to higher computational load. One remarkable exception is Maji et al. (2008) who approximate the histogram intersection kernel for faster execution. Their proposed approximation is used in our experiments as well.

AdaBoost. Contrary to SVMs, boosting algorithms (Friedman et al., 2000) optimize the classification error on the training samples iteratively. Each round a weak classifier is chosen in order to optimally reduce the training error. The weighted sum of all weak classifiers forms the final strong classifier. A typical choice for weak learners, which are required to do better than chance, are decision tree stumps operating on a single dimension of the feature vector. In this work, we use AdaBoost as formulated by Viola and Jones (2004).

MPLBoost. MPLBoost (Babenko et al., 2008) or MCBoost as called by Kim and Cipolla (2008) is a recently proposed extension to AdaBoost. While AdaBoost fails to learn a classifier where positive samples appear in multiple clusters arranged in an XOR-like layout, MPLBoost successfully manages this learning problem. This is achieved by simultaneously learning K strong classifiers, while the response to an input pattern is given as the maximum response of all K strong classifiers. Thus, a window is classified as positive if a single strong classifier yields a positive score and negative only if all strong classifiers consider the window as negative. Also the runtime is only linear in the number of weak classifiers. During learning positive samples that are misclassified by all strong classifiers obtain a high weight, while positive samples which are classified correctly by a single strong classifier are assigned a low weight. This enables the learning algorithm to focus on a subpart of misclassified data (up to the current round) with a single strong classifier. Other strong classifiers are not affected and therefore do not loose their discriminative power on their specific clusters learned.

4.3 LEARNING AND TESTING

While features and classifiers are the key components of the detectors several issues need to be taken care of for both learning and testing. Those details are often crucial to obtain best performance, even though they are seldom discussed in literature. The following sections give some detailed insights on our learning (Section 4.3.1) and testing procedure (Section 4.3.2).

4.3.1 Improved learning procedure

Our classifiers are trained in a two-step bootstrapping process. In order to improve the statistics of hard examples for the domain where pedestrians actually appear, the negative test set also contains frames from an onboard camera recorded in an urban area. Those are scanned for hard examples, but detections that are close to a pedestrian in x-y-$scale$-space are considered true positive. The minimal distance is chosen such that detections on body parts are allowed as hard examples.

Often these types of false positives are not well represented in other detectors' training data. Figure 4.4(a) shows highest scoring false positive detections in the bootstrapping phase after removing the full detections, showing that body parts are indeed hard examples for the initial detector.

Additionally, we found that merging the false positive detections on the negative images by mean shift is beneficial in several ways. First, the variability of false positive detections for the second round of training can be increased and the space of negative samples is covered well, while keeping the memory requirements reasonable. Second,

4.3 LEARNING AND TESTING

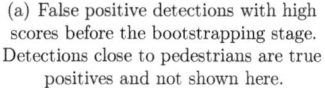

(a) False positive detections with high scores before the bootstrapping stage. Detections close to pedestrians are true positives and not shown here.

(b) Visualization color coding for flow direction and magnitude

Figure 4.3: Bootstrapping from false detections on parts and optic flow color coding

false positive regions with a larger number of false detections are not over-counted since they will only be contained once in the training set and thus have the same weight as regions on which the detectors only fires a few times. This is consistent with the fact that for real-world systems the optimal image-based performance is sought and all false detections should be treated equally.

4.3.2 Testing

As it is desirable for real-world applications to detect pedestrians as soon as possible we are aiming to detect pedestrians as small as possible. Empirically we found that given appropriate image quality upscaling the input image allows for a better performance gain with respect to small detections than shrinking the detection window (cf. Figure 4.3(b)). Therefore, we upscale the input image by a factor of two which allows to detect pedestrians as small as 48 pixels with a 64×128 pixel detection window (the window contains context in addition to the pedestrian). Sliding window based detection systems usually fire multiple times on true pedestrians on nearby positions in scale and space. These detections need to be merged in order to allow for a per-image based evaluation such as false positive per image (FPPI) or precision and recall (PR). Here, we adopt an adapted bandwidth mean-shift based mode seeking strategy (Comaniciu, 2003) to determine the position in x-y-$scale$-space, but determine the final detection's score to be the maximum of all scores within the mode. While others (e.g., Dalal, 2006) have used the kernel density to form the final score, we found the maximum to provide more robust results. While most of the time the performance is comparable, in some cases choosing the kernel density leads to a significantly decreased performance in particular for the motion-enhanced detector (cf. Figure 4.10(f)). Another important issue is the estimation of the kernel density – in a scale pyramid setting with a constant pixel stride for every scale, detections on larger scales are sparser. Thus, contrary to Dalal (2006) when computing the kernel density we omit the kernel volume's scale adaption for the normalization factor.

4.4 NEW DATASET

To the best of our knowledge the sequences of Ess *et al.* (2007, 2008) were (when we originally conducted this work) the only publicly available video sequences for pedestrian detection recorded from a moving platform. While those are realistic for robotics scenarios, they are less realistic for automotive safety applications. This is mainly due to the relatively small ego-motion and the camera's field of view which is focusing on the near range. In order to show results for a more realistic and challenging automotive safety scenario in urban environment, we captured a new onboard dataset (*TUD-Brussels*) from a driving car.

At the same time there is no dedicated training set containing temporal image pairs that has sufficient variability to train a discriminative detector based on motion features. Thus, we additionally recorded a new training dataset (*TUD-MotionPairs*) containing pairs of images to compute optical flow. Both new datasets are made publicly available[7].

Training sets. Our new positive training set (*TUD-MotionPairs*) consists of 1092 image pairs with 1776 annotated pedestrians (resulting in 3552 positive samples with mirroring), recorded from a hand-held camera at a resolution of 720 × 576 pixels. The images are recorded in busy pedestrian zones. Some samples are shown in Figure 4.4. Note that contrary to the database of Dalal and Triggs (2005) ours is not restricted to upright standing pedestrians but also contains pedestrians from side views which are particularly relevant in applications due to the possibility of crossing the camera's own trajectory.

Our negative training set consists of 192 image pairs. 85 image pairs were recorded in an inner city district, using the same camera as was used for the positive dataset at a resolution of 720 × 576 pixels, while another 107 image pairs were recorded from a moving car. For finding body parts as hard samples as described in Section 4.3.1 we use an additional set of 26 image pairs, recorded from a moving vehicle containing 183 pedestrian annotations. We use this training set for all experiments throughout this chapter.

Test sets. The new *TUD-Brussels* dataset is recorded from a driving car in the inner city of Brussels. The set contains 508 image pairs (one pair per second and its successor of the original video) at a resolution of 640 × 480 with overall 1326 annotated pedestrians. The dataset is challenging due to the fact that pedestrians appear from multiple viewpoints and at very small scales. Additionally, many pedestrians are partially occluded (mostly by cars) and the background is cluttered (e.g., poles, parking cars and buildings and people crowds) as typical for busy city districts. The use of motion information is complicated not only by the fact that the camera is moving, but also by

---

[7]http://www.mis.informatik.tu-darmstadt.de

Figure 4.4: Positive sample crops and flow fields of *TUD-MotionPairs*

the facts, that the speed is varying and the car is turning. Some sample views are given in Figure 4.1.

Additionally we evaluate our detectors on the publicly available ETH-Person (Ess et al., 2007) dataset. Ess et al. (2007) presented three datasets of 640 × 480 pixel stereo images recorded in a pedestrian zone from a moving stroller. The camera is moving forward at a moderate speed with only minor rotation. The sets contain 999, 450 and 354 consecutive frames of the left camera and 5193, 2359 and 1828 annotations respectively. As our detector detected many pedestrians below the minimum annotation height in these sets, we complemented the sets with annotations for the smaller pedestrians. Thus, all pedestrians with a height of at least 48 pixels are considered for our evaluation.

4.5 RESULTS

Since we are interested in performance on a system level we refrain from evaluation in terms of FPPW but present plots in terms of recall and precision. This allows a better assessment of the detector as the entire detector pipeline is evaluated rather than the feature and classifier in isolation (cf. Dollár et al., 2009b). As a common reference point we will report the obtained recall at a precision of 90%. We also show plots of false positives per image to compare with previous work (i.e., Ess et al., 2007). We start the discussion of results with the static image descriptors and then discuss the benefit of adding motion features.

Results for the static features are given in the first row of Figures 4.8 and 4.9. In combination with the HOG feature MPLBoost significantly outperforms AdaBoost on all tested sequences. In detail the improvement in recall at 90% precision is: 27.7% on ETH-01 (Figure 4.9(a)), 24.4% on ETH-02 (Figure 4.9(b)), 41.1% on ETH-03 (Figure 4.10(a)) and 20.3% on *TUD-Brussels* (Figure 4.10(b)). Also it can be observed that HOG features in combination with MPLBoost do better than HOG features in combination with a linear SVM on all four datasets. The gain in detail in recall at 90% precision is: 8.5% on ETH-01 (Figure 4.9(a)), 4.9% on ETH-02 (Figure 4.9(b)), 22.6% on ETH-03 (Figure 4.10(a)) and 2.0% on *TUD-Brussels* (Figure 4.10(b)). Compared to a SVM with histogram intersection kernel (HIKSVM) the results are divergent. While

Figure 4.5: Optic flow fields (top row) and sample detections on the *TUD-Brussels* onboard dataset at equal error rate for HOG, Haar, IMHwd and MPLBoost(K=4) (middle row) and HOG, Haar, IMHwd and SVM (bottom row). True positives are yellow, false positives red.

HIKSVM outperforms MPLBoost by 1.4% on *TUD-Brussels* (Figure 4.10(b)) and by 0.4% on ETH-01 (Figure 4.9(a)), on ETH-02 and ETH-03 MPLBoost performs better by 1.9% (Figure 4.9(b)) and 12.9% (Figure 4.10(a)) respectively.

Next we turn to the results with HOG and Haar features in combination with different classifiers. On the *TUD-Brussels* dataset (Figure 4.10(b)) we observe an improvement of 0.3% at 90% precision for MPLBoost, while on equal error rate (EER) the improvement is 4.3%. For the ETH databases we yield equal or slightly worse results compared to the detectors with HOG features only (Figures 4.9(a), (b) and 4.10(a)). Closer inspection revealed minor image quality (cf. Figure 4.6) with respect to colors and lighting on the ETH databases to be problematic, impeding a performance improvement (cf. Figures 4.9(a), (b) and 4.10(a)). Haar wavelets computed on color channels are not robust enough to these imaging conditions. Note however, that MPLBoost outperforms linear SVM, HIKSVM and AdaBoost for this feature combination showing its applicability for pedestrian detection. HIKSVM consistently obtained worse results with Haar features for static as well as for motion-enhanced detectors. Hence, these plots are omitted for better readability.

We continue to analyze the performance when IMHwd motion features in combination with HOG features are used for detection. The resulting plots are depicted in the second

Figure 4.6: Sample detections at 0.5 FPPI on ETH-Person dataset (top row: Optic flow field of Zach *et al.* (2007), middle row: System of Ess *et al.* (2007), bottom row: Our motion-enhanced detector). Columns 1-3 correspond to Figures 4.9(e), (f) and 4.10(e) respectively, however all detections (even those smaller than 70 pixels) are shown. Note the false positive in the lower right image is actually a reflection of a true pedestrian.

row of Figures 4.8 and 4.9. For HIKSVM we observe a consistent improvement over the best static image detector. In detail the improvement at a precision of 90% precision is: 3.7% on ETH-01 (Figure 4.9(c)), 16.9% on ETH-02 (Figure 4.9(d)), 2.2% on ETH-03 (Figure 4.10(c)) and 14.0% on *TUD-Brussels* (Figure 4.10(d)). In contrast to Dalal (2006) we can clearly show a significant performance gain using motion features. The difference in performance however depends on the dataset and the distribution of viewpoints in the test sets. More specifically motion is beneficial mostly for side views but also for 45-degrees views whereas front-back views profit less from the added motion features.

This explains the lower performance gain for ETH-01 (Figure 4.9(c)) and ETH-03 (Figure 4.10(c)) which are dominated by front-back views. We also observe that linear SVMs perform about as good as MPLBoost for this feature combination, while HIKSVM does better than both except for ETH-03. Sample detections for MPLBoost and linear SVMs are shown in Figure 4.5. Note that false detections differ between both classifiers. While MPLBoost tends to fire on high frequency background structure, SVMs tend to fire more often on pedestrian-like structures such as poles. We explain the similar overall performance by the fact that motion features allow a good linear separability in

Figure 4.7: Sample detections for the different models learned by MPLBoost (K=4) using HOG, Haar, IMHwd. The models to the left respond more strongly to side/45-degree views, the models to the right to front/back views.

particular for side-views. This is consistent with our observation that MPLBoost mainly uses appearance features for the clusters firing on front-back views and more IMHwd features for clusters which fire on side views. Additionally, MPLBoost and SVMs again clearly outperform AdaBoost.

Combining IMHwd and HOG features additionally with Haar features yields similar results as for the static case with only little changes for MPLBoost. Interestingly linear SVMs obtain a better precision on *TUD-Brussels* for this combination, but loose performance on the ETH sequences as discussed for the static detectors. More sophisticated feature combination schemes (e.g., Varma and Ray, 2007) may allow to improve performance more consistently based on multiple features.

We have also analyzed the viewpoints different MPLBoost classifiers fire on. Figure 4.7 depicts the two highest scoring detections on *TUD-Brussels* of the detector using HOG, IMHwd and Haar features for each of the four clusters. Clearly, two clusters predominantly fire on side and 45-degree side views while two clusters mostly detect pedestrians from front-back views.

Additionally, we investigate the achieved recall for pedestrians on different scales. Figure 4.10 shows the obtained recall with and without motion features at a precision of 90% for the *TUD-Brussels* dataset. It can be seen that in particular detection on small scales improves by adding motion features.

Finally, we compare our detector to the system of Ess *et al.* (2007) (last row of Figures 4.8 and 4.9). The original authors kindly provided us with their system's output in order to allow for a fair comparison based on the modified set of annotations. For each sequence we plot the best performance of a static image feature detector and of the best detector including motion features. We consistently outperform Ess *et al.* (2007) on all three sequences without any refinement of detections by the estimation of a ground plane. This refinement could obviously be added and would allow for further improvement. At 0.5 false positives per image we improve recall compared to their system by: 18.6% on ETH-01 (Figure 4.9(e)), 32.2% on ETH-02 (Figure 4.9(f)) and 37.3% on ETH-03 (Figure 4.10(e)). To keep this comparison fair, we only considered pedestrians larger than 70 pixels similar to the original evaluation setting. Also note that HIKSVM with motion features clearly outperforms MPLBoost, while both classifiers are almost on par when all pedestrians as small as 48 pixels are considered. We also outperform Zhang *et al.* (2008) who report 64.3% recall at 1.5 FFPI even though their detector is trained

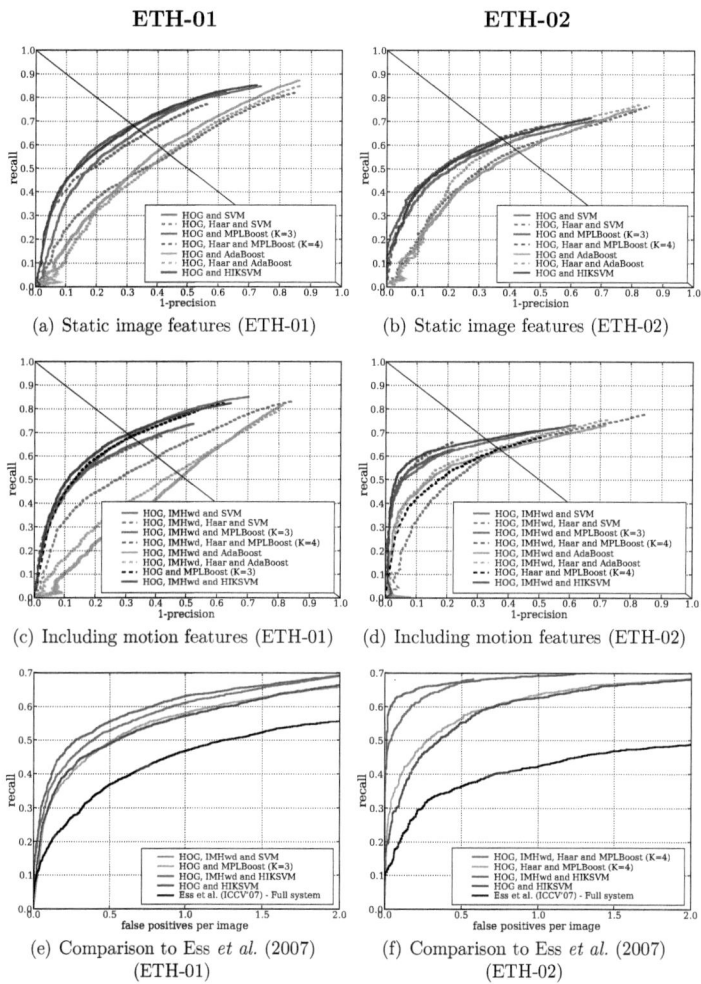

Figure 4.8: Results obtained with different combinations of features and classifiers on ETH-01 and ETH-02 (Ess et al., 2007). Note that first and second row show details on static and motion features in combination with different classifiers considering all detections larger than 48 pixels with recall and precision as metric. Row three compares our detector to the system of Ess et al. (2007) (only pedestrians larger than 70 pixel are considered, evaluation in FPPI).

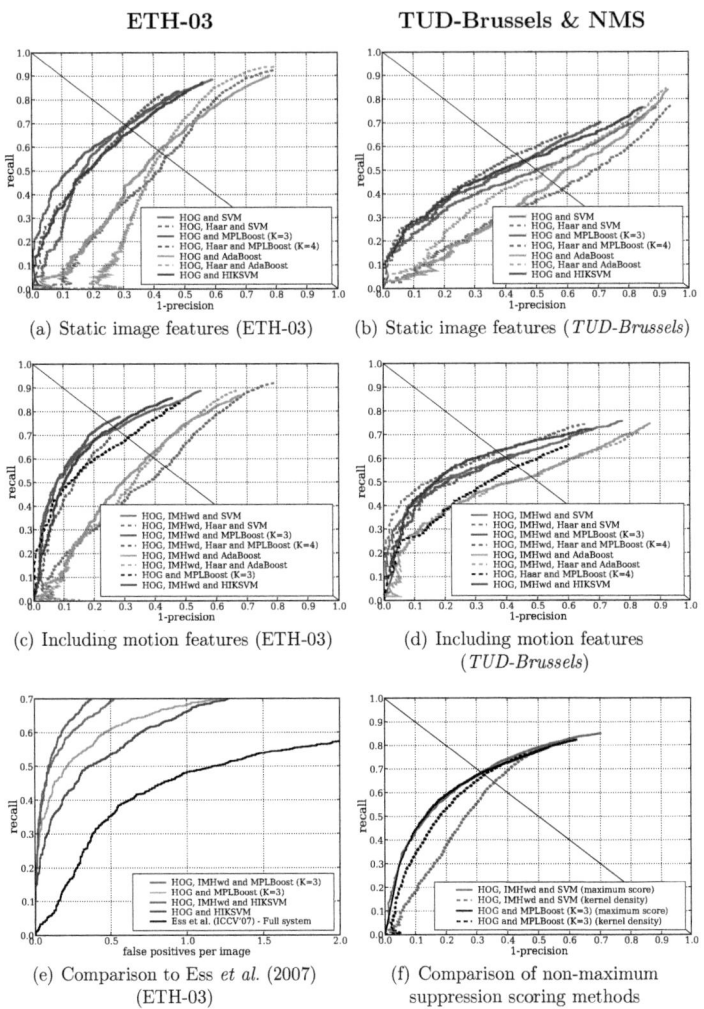

Figure 4.9: Results obtained with different combinations of features and classifiers on ETH-03 (Ess *et al.*, 2007) and *TUD-Brussels*. Note that first and second row show details on static and motion features in combination with different classifiers considering all detections larger than 48 pixels with recall and precision as metric. Row three compares our detector to the system of Ess *et al.* (2007) (only pedestrians larger than 70 pixel are considered, evaluation in FPPI) and shows a comparison of different non-maximum suppression approaches (Figure 4.10(f)).

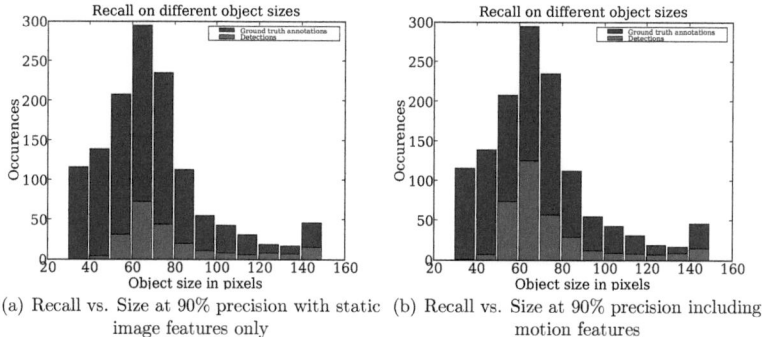

(a) Recall vs. Size at 90% precision with static image features only

(b) Recall vs. Size at 90% precision including motion features

Figure 4.10: Comparison of recall for different pedestrian sizes at a precision of 90%

on ETH-02 and ETH-03 whereas our detector is trained on an independent and more general multi-view training set. Sample detections of our detector as well as system results of Ess et al. (2007) are shown in Figure 4.6. Note that our detector can detect very small pedestrians and achieves better recall throughout all scales by exploiting motion information.

4.6 CONCLUSION

In this chapter we tackled the challenging task of detecting pedestrians seen from multiple views from a moving car by using multiple appearance features as well as motion features. We show that HIKSVM and MPLBoost achieve superior performance to linear SVM-based detectors for static multi-viewpoint pedestrian detection. Moreover, both significantly outperform AdaBoost on this task. When additional motion features are used, HIKSVMs perform best while MPLBoost performs as good as linear SVMs but in any case better than AdaBoost. In general however, MPLBoost seemed to be the most robust classifier with respect to challenging lighting conditions while being computationally less expensive than SVMs.

Additionally, our careful design of the learning and testing procedures improves detection performance on a per-image measure substantially when the IMHwd motion features of Dalal et al. (2006) are used which has been identified as an open problem in Dalal (2006). This improvement is observed for pedestrians at all scales but particularly for side views which are of high importance for automotive safety applications, since those pedestrians tend to cross the car's trajectory. Additionally, we show (contrary to Dalal et al., 2006) that regularized flows (Zach et al., 2007), allow to improve detection performance. Adding additional Haar wavelets as features allowed to improve detection performance in some cases, but in general we observe that the feature is quite sensitive to varying cameras and lighting conditions.

Temporal integration by means of tracking over multiple frames will help to bridge missing detections while a more complete scene analysis featuring 3D scene understanding (see Chapter 7) will help to prune false positive detections. For future work, we will further investigate ways of encoding motion information in an ego-motion invariant way. Also we are planning to work on the issue of partial occlusion, which is a prominent drawback of global object descriptors.

5
REAL-TIME OBJECT DETECTION

Contents

5.1	Introduction	**71**
5.2	Object class detection using HOG	**72**
5.3	Programming on the GPU	**73**
5.4	HOG on the GPU	**74**
5.5	Discussion on GPU implementations	**77**
5.6	Experiments	**79**
	5.6.1 Datasets	79
	5.6.2 Detection performance	81
	5.6.3 Runtime analysis	82
5.7	Conclusion	**84**

W HILE Chapter 3 and Chapter 4 focused on a systematic evaluation and improvement of object detectors, this chapter is concentrating on improving the processing speed of a state-of-the-art object detection system. Processing speed is a particular issue for highly dynamic application environments as for instance in automotive scenarios. Even in urban areas where a driving speed of around 50 km/h (30 miles/h) can be assumed, frame rates of around 10-20 Hz are required to achieve a satisfying overall system performance.

However, state-of-the-art object detectors (see for instance Chapter 3 and Chapter 4) require processing times in the order of multiple seconds on a standard CPU. Thus, in this chapter we argue that massive parallelism for feature computation and for the sliding window framework can be exploited to achieve the required frame rates for a state-of-the-art detector (Dalal and Triggs, 2005) on standard graphics hardware (GPUs).

Contrary to related work (Zhang *et al.*, 2007; Zhu *et al.*, 2006) we do not sacrifice detection performance in order to achieve real-time speed. In our experiments we show equal performance of our GPU implementation to existing CPU implementations for people and car detection but at a frame rate of several Hz.

5.1 INTRODUCTION

In recent literature, densely sampled local descriptors have shown excellent performance, and therefore have become more and more popular for object class recognition. As the processing power of computers increases, sliding window-based techniques become more and more feasible for real-time applications.

While interest point detectors offer a smart way for pre-sampling possible locations and therefore provide a sparser set for learning and recognition, the advantage of dense random sampling, or sampling on a regular lattice has been shown (Nowak et al., 2006; Tuytelaars and Schmid, 2007) to outperform sparse representations. Many of the best object class detectors use sliding window techniques (e.g., Papageorgiou and Poggio, 2000; Viola and Jones, 2004; Shashua et al., 2004; Dalal and Triggs, 2005; Laptev, 2006; Tuzel et al., 2007), i.e., extract overlapping detection windows at each possible position, or on a regular lattice, and evaluate a classifier. The sliding window technique is, in general, often criticized as being too resource intensive, and consequently, it is often seen as unfeasible for real-time systems. However, many high dynamic automotive applications are interested in detecting pedestrians using this technique in a fast and yet robust manner (Gavrila and Philomin, 1999; Shashua et al., 2004; Munder and Gavrila, 2006). In general, gradient based methods (Shashua et al., 2004; Dalal and Triggs, 2005; Laptev, 2006; Tuzel et al., 2007) perform very well, but most of them are computationally expensive.

The ideal solution is to avoid rejection phases relying on coarser features, downscaled images, or other approximations, and to process the entire detection window with a strong, high-resolution classifier. In this chapter we argue that methods that sacrifice classification performance in order to achieve speed-ups, do not stand in the long term. We show that by using parallel architectures that can be found in many recent PC's graphics processors (GPUs) we can easily obtain a speed-up of 30 and more. As a case study, we present an implementation of Dalal and Triggs (2005) Histograms of oriented gradients (HOG) approach using a technology called general-purpose computation on graphics processing units (GPGPU). Our performance analysis shows guidelines for better optimization, and how to avoid unnecessary overhead using GPGPU technology.

The remainder of this chapter is structured as follows. Section 5.2 will give a brief introduction to object class detection using HOG features. Section 5.3 will introduce this work's GPU programming model, while Section 5.4 reports details of our implementation. Section 5.5 provides a more general discussion about GPGPU programming techniques. Section 5.6 shows several experiments regarding both detection and runtime performance. We conclude this chapter with Section 5.7.

5.2 OBJECT CLASS DETECTION USING HOG

This section provides a brief overview of object class detection using HOG (Dalal and Triggs, 2005) features. All provided parameters correspond to experiments on people detection, and are similar to Dalal and Triggs (2005).

Detection phase. A given test image is scanned at all scales and locations. The ratio between the scales is 1.05, and the overlapping detection windows are extracted with a step size of 8 pixels, both horizontally and vertically. HOG features are computed for each detection window, and a linear SVM classifier decides upon the presence of the object class. Finally, a robust mode estimator, a mean shift algorithm (Comaniciu, 2003), fuses multiple detections over position and scale space (3D), and the system returns bounding boxes marked by their confidence.

Figure 5.2(a) illustrates the computation of a rectangular HOG feature for a given detection window. After image normalization and gradient computation, each detection window is divided into adjacent cells of 8×8 pixels. Each cell is represented by a 9-bin histogram of gradient orientations in the range of $0° - 180°$, weighted by their magnitudes. A group of 2×2 cells is called a block. Blocks are overlapping, and are normalized using L_2-Hys, the Lowe-style clipped L_2 norm. A block is represented as a concatenation of all cell histograms, and a HOG feature as a concatenation of all blocks. For people, 64×128 pixels is a common choice for the detection window size. When blocks overlap 50%, i.e., 1 cell – which is a typical choice for efficient CPU implementations – a detection window consists of $7 \times 15 = 105$ blocks, and therefore the length of a HOG descriptor is $105 \times 2 \times 2 \times 9 = 3780$. To be robust to small translations, cell histograms are computed with tri-linear interpolation. Gradient magnitudes are weighted by a Gaussian ($\sigma = 8.0$) centered at the middle of the given block. In case of color images, channels are separated, and orientation histograms are built using the maximum gradient of the channels.

Learning phase. The HOG descriptors are computed similarly to detection. The learning phase differs in that there is neither need to compute the full scale-space for all images, nor to scan the images with a sliding window. Using the given annotations, normalized crops of fixed resolution are created and fed into SVM training. Negative crops are first chosen at random, or given by the dataset. After training an initial SVM classifier a bootstrapping stage is employed. The negative images are scanned for false positives to create "hard examples" and retrain the SVM – a typical technique to improve the classifier by one order of magnitude (Munder and Gavrila, 2006).

5.3 PROGRAMMING ON THE GPU

The term GPGPU refers to a technique that uses the graphics chip as a co-processor to perform scientific computations. The architecture of GPUs allows highly parallel computations at high speed, and thus provides an excellent platform for computer vision. GPU manufacturers have realized the need for better support of non-graphics applications, and therefore they have been working on novel architectures. In this chapter our implementation is based on NVIDIA's CUDA architecture and programming model. Consequently, we use a CUDA capable card, GeForce 8800 Ultra, for our experiments. All numbers and speed measurements in this chapter reflect this model. While CUDA allows us to use typical computer graphics procedures, such as vertex and fragment shaders, algorithms still need to be adapted to achieve high data level parallelism, and efficient memory access.

The graphics card GeForce 8800 Ultra, a highly multi-threaded device, consists of 16 multi-processors, each one made up of 8 processors, and therefore, capable of running 128 *threads* simultaneously. Current state-of-the-art models (e.g., GeForce GTX 480) that appeared after we originally published this work can run up to 480 threads in parallel and will therefore achieve an additional speed-up. Programs running on the

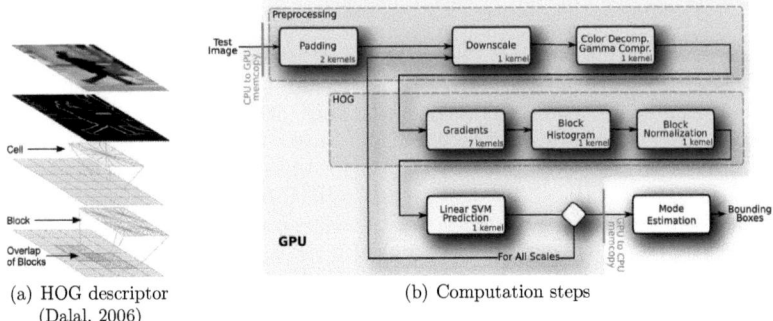

(a) HOG descriptor (Dalal, 2006) (b) Computation steps

Figure 5.1: Sliding window object localization using HOG descriptors

GPU, called *kernels*, are compiled with NVIDIA's C compiler. Kernels are launched with a user specified *grid* and *thread block* configuration. Thread blocks group up to 512 threads together, and are arranged in a grid to help complex addressing. Each block runs on the same multi-processor and therefore may share data, via on-chip *shared memories*. Each multi-processor has 8192 registers and 16384 bytes of shared memory that are dynamically allocated to threads and thread blocks.

Due to these limitations and the configuration of threads, not all processors can be active all the time. The ratio that reflects how a kernel occupies the GPU is called the *occupancy* and is 100% at best. In general, higher occupancy hides the latency of global memory accesses better, and therefore often leads to better performance.

Besides the on-chip shared memory there are three other types of off-chip memories. The *global memory* (768MB), also called device memory, has high latency and is not cached. *Constant memory* (65536 bytes) is typically used if all threads are accessing the same pre-computed value, and *texture memory* (65536 bytes) is optimized for 2D spatial locality. Constant and texture memories are transparently cached (8KB on-chip). Each type of memory has different access patterns, and thus programmers have to decide where the data is stored for best performance. E.g., the high-latency global memory is best accessed in continuous chunks that are aligned w.r.t. thread blocks. This is the so-called *coalesced memory access*.

5.4 HOG on the GPU

Figure 5.2(b) shows the steps of our implementation. First, the image is transferred from the CPU's main memory to the GPU's global memory. After initial padding, the test image is gradually downscaled, and for each scale the HOG descriptor is computed on the color normalized channels. A linear SVM is evaluated and the scores are transferred back to the CPU's memory for non-maximum suppression. Training of the SVM is done on the CPU with fixed image crops (Section 5.6), but using the GPU implementation to

5.4 HOG ON THE GPU

extract HOGs. In the following we detail the steps of our detector.

Preprocessing. Preprocessing consists of four steps. In order to detect objects that are partially cropped or near the image boundaries, extra padding is added to each side of the image. Then, the image is gradually downscaled, color channels are separated, and on each channel a color normalization is performed. In the following we discuss the implementation of each step.

Padding. After a test image is transferred to the global memory of the GPU, extra pixels are added to each side of the image. Each new pixel is computed by averaging the color of the closest 5 pixels in the previous row/column.

The implementation is split into two, vertical and horizontal, kernels while for each two thread blocks are launched. Due to the pixel dependencies from previous computations, kernels compute the missing pixels in a row/column-wise manner. Our implementation loads an entire row/column into the shared memory (max. 16KB), imposing a reasonable limit on target image dimensions, 2038 pixels. Due to the limitation on the number of registers the kernel occupancy is at most 42% as indicated in Table 5.1.

Downscale. Our downscale kernel takes advantage of the texturing unit to efficiently subsample the source image by a factor of 1.05 using linear interpolation. The target image is "covered" by thread blocks which consist of 16×16 threads. Each thread computes one pixel of the downscaled image.

Color decomposition & gamma compression. This kernel's purpose is to separate the color channels of a 32-bit color interleaved image to red, green, and blue. The target pixels of the decomposed channels are also converted to floats, for further processing. Each thread corresponds to a pixel, and for efficient memory access they are grouped into 16×16 thread blocks. Since gamma compression also is a pixel-wise operation, it is integrated into this kernel for best performance, i.e., to save unnecessary kernel launches.

Color gradients. Separable convolution kernels (from the SDK examples) compute x and y derivatives of each color channel ($3 * 2$ kernel launches). According to the guidelines, thread block sizes are fixed to 145 and 128 threads for horizontal and vertical convolutions, respectively. The occupancy is bounded by these numbers, and is 83% for horizontal and 67% for vertical processing (cf. Table 5.1).

The next kernel computes gradient orientations and magnitudes. Each thread is responsible for computing one pixel taken as a maximum of the gradient on the three channels. For efficiency threads are grouped in 16×16 blocks.

Kernel	Registers	Sh.Mem.	Thrd/Blk	Occupancy	Coal. mem.
Padding	22	$80 + D$	320	max. 42%	Only vert.
Downscale	9	40	16×16	100%	Yes
Color Decomposition, Gamma compression	7	72	16×16	100%	Yes
Horizontal Convolution	6	556	**145**	83%	Yes
Vertical Convolution	**15**	**3244**	16×8	67%	Yes
Gradient Orientation Magnitude - Max	13	60	16×16	67%	Yes
Block Histograms	13	**2468**	16×4	50%	Yes
Block Normalization	5	312	**36**	67%	No
Linear SVM Evaluation	**15**	1072	128	67%	Yes

Table 5.1: Maximum occupancy per kernel is determined by the number of registers, amount of shared memory (in bytes), and the thread block configuration. Bold numbers indicate the current limitation. Padding needs additional shared memory D, see text for details. The last column shows whether the kernel has fully coalesced memory access. Figures correspond to detector settings for people detection.

Block histograms. Our implementation is inspired by the `histogram64` example[8]. The basic idea of parallel histogram computation is to store partial results, so-called sub-histograms, in the low-latency shared memory. If the number of histogram bins per cell, h_c is 9, our algorithm requires $h_c * sizeof(\text{float}) = 9 * 4 = 36$ bytes of shared memory per thread. There are two pre-computed tables, Gaussian weights and bilinear spatial weighting, transferred to the texture memory. Interpolation between the orientation bin centers is computed in the kernel. Assuming HOG block size of 2×2 cells, and 8×8-pixel cell sizes, the Gaussian weights require $16 * 16 * 4 = 1024$ bytes, and the bilinear weighting table needs $16 * 16 * 2 * 4 = 4096$ bytes.

Each thread block is responsible for the computation of one HOG block. Threads within a block are logically grouped, such that each group computes one cell histogram, and each thread processes one column of gradient orientation and magnitude values corresponding to the HOG block. Given the above mentioned cell and block sizes, in our case a thread block has 16×4 threads. This arrangement reflects the cell structure within a HOG block, and therefore provides easier indexing to our pre-computed tables.

The second part of the kernel fuses the sub-histograms to a single HOG block histogram using the same technique as `histogram64`[9]. Our configuration runs with 50% GPU occupancy, due to size limits on shared memory (cf. Table 5.1).

---

[8]NVIDIA CUDA SDK Code Samples: http://developer.download.nvidia.com/compute/cuda/sdk/website/samples.html#histogram

[9]NVIDIA CUDA SDK Code Samples: http://developer.download.nvidia.com/compute/cuda/sdk/website/samples.html#histogram

Block normalization. HOG blocks are normalized individually using L_2-Hys by a kernel, where each thread block is responsible to normalize one HOG block, and consists of the number of histogram bins per block, h_b, threads. For people detection we set $h_b = 9$ for car detection we use $h_b = 18$. Squaring of the individual elements as well as the sum of the squares are computed in parallel. Keeping a full HOG block in shared memory avoids the latency of global memory accesses. The kernel runs with 67% occupancy (cf. Table 5.1).

Linear SVM evaluation. This kernel is similar to the block normalization kernel, since both are based on a dot product, and therefore inspired by the example scalarProd[10]. Each thread block is responsible for one detection window. Each thread in a block computes weighted sums corresponding to each column of the window. Partial sums are added in a pairwise element fashion, at each time using half of the threads until only one thread is left running. Finally, the bias of the hyperplane is subtracted and the distance from the margin is stored in global memory. The number of threads per block is 128.

During computation, the linear weights of the trained SVM are kept in texture memory. Keeping all values of a detection window in shared memory would occupy nearly all available space, therefore we have decided to store one partial result of the dot product for each thread, $128 * 4 = 512$ bytes. The kernel runs with 67% GPU occupancy (cf. Table 5.1).

Non-maximum suppression. The window-wise classification is insensitive to small changes in scale and position. Thus, the detector naturally fires multiple times at nearby scale and space positions. To obtain a single final hypothesis for each object, these detections are fused with a non-maximum suppression algorithm, a scale adaptive bandwidth mean shift (Comaniciu, 2003).

This algorithm is currently running on the CPU. Our current time estimates suggest that it is not yet worth to run it on the GPU. However, parallelization of kernel density estimates with mode searching could itself be a research topic. In the future, we plan to run the estimation on the CPU asynchronously and simultaneously to the other computations on the GPU.

5.5 DISCUSSION ON GPU IMPLEMENTATIONS

This section summarizes our general experience for porting existing computer vision techniques to the GPU. The following guidelines should give an impression for what is worth, and what is hard to realize on GPU architectures.

Port complete sequence of operations to the GPU. Due to the transfer overhead between the CPU and the GPU, it is not profitable to port only small portions of

---

[10] NVIDIA CUDA SDK Code Samples: http://developer.download.nvidia.com/compute/cuda/sdk/website/samples.html#scalarProd

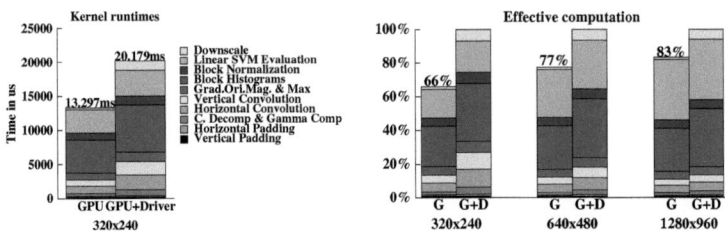

Figure 5.2: Effective GPU times and calling overheads. See text for details.

a complete framework to the GPU. E.g., just to run convolution on the GPU and do the rest on the CPU involves an overhead twice as much as the effective computation on the GPU. It is better to keep the data on the GPU for further processing, in particular, if we can further compress it. E.g., our transfer time of all SVM results currently takes 0.430ms even for a large image of 1280×960, however, transferring back all HOG descriptors would have taken 2 to 3 orders of magnitude more time.

Group subsequent steps together. Our experience has shown that integrating kernels that access the data in the same fashion leads to significant speed improvements due to the reduced number of kernel launches. E.g., if we split the decompose colors & gamma compression, or the gradient orientation & maximum selection kernels into two, our algorithm slows down by 2ms for each. Figure 5.2 (left) shows that the GPU computation time for an image of size 320×240 is 13.297ms, and the program actually spends 20.179ms in the driver software, which includes the effective GPU time and the additional overhead of kernel launches and parameter passing.

Larger data, higher speed-up. Consequently, the more data we process, the larger is the expected speed-up compared to a CPU implementation. Notice that the overhead is independent of the GPU time, and in case of longer computations, it could be relatively small. Figure 5.2 (right) shows the real GPU computation in relation to the kernel running time, including overhead, on different image sizes. While for a smaller image the overhead is 34% for a larger image it is only 17%.

Choose the right memory type. Different memory types have different access patterns. It is important to choose the right one. E.g., the SVM evaluation may store the SVM weights in constant memory. However, since each thread accesses a different weight, it is better to use the texture memory. In our case SVM evaluation speeds up by a factor of 1.6, i.e., by 3ms for a 320×240 image using the texture memory. Similarly another 3ms is won by storing the pre-computed Gaussian weights in the texture memory for the histogram computation.

Address aligned data. Alignment guidelines are essential for global memory access. In simple cases this usually means additional padding of images. For more complicated cases, when the same data is accessed multiple times using different patterns, the threads have to be aligned on the data, e.g., by launching more threads, and according to the alignment some of them do nothing. Our experience has shown that non-coalesced global memory access may cause a slowdown of kernels of up to 10 times.

Flexibility has high impact on speed. Due to the above guidelines, flexibility, i.e., using not hard-coded parameters can cause significant slowdown by, e.g., non-coalesced memory access, or by increasing kernel launch overhead due to more parameters, or by more variables and computations that increase the number of registers and the amount of required shared memory, and consequently reducing occupancy.

Launch many threads to scale for the future. Finally, to scale well for future improvements of hardware a good implementation launches thousands of threads simultaneously, even if only 128 run physically parallel on the current cards.

Due to the above overheads, the sub-optimal memory access, and the rest of the computation, loading/saving, etc., one can only expect an actual speed-up of a magnitude less than 128. In the following section we report real WALL times for our experiments, and measure the actual speed-up of our HOG implementation.

5.6 EXPERIMENTS

In order to verify both performance and runtime of our implementation we conducted several experiments on the INRIA Person test set (Dalal and Triggs, 2005) for pedestrian detection. Moreover, we evaluated the performance for car detection on the TUD Dynamic Scenes (TUDDS) dataset (Wojek and Schiele, 2008a).

For evaluation we use precision-recall curves, which provide a more intuitive and more informative report than false positives per window (FPPW) statistics on the performance of object localization. FPPW plots do not reflect the distribution of false positives in scale and location space, i.e., how the classifier performs in the vicinity of objects, or on background that is similar to the object context.

As described earlier our system has a non-maximum suppression step to merge nearby detections to one final hypothesis, and therefore providing a clear way for evaluation. Detections are counted as true positives if they match the ground truth annotations with less than 50% overlap error, and double detections are counted as false positives, according to the PASCAL (Everingham *et al.*, 2010) criteria.

5.6.1 Datasets

The INRIA Person dataset contains people in different challenging scenes. For training, the dataset contains 2416 normalized positive (i.e., people cropped from 615 images) and 1218 negative images. For testing the dataset has 453 negative images, a set of 1132 positive crops, and their corresponding 288 full size images. Some sample images are shown in Figure 5.3.

Figure 5.3: Sample detections on the INRIA Person dataset

Figure 5.4: Sample detections on the TUD Dynamic Scenes (TUDDS) dataset

5.6 EXPERIMENTS

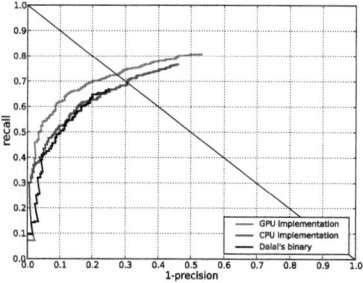

Implementation	WALL time
Dalal's binary	39 min 28s
Our CPU	35 min 1s
Our GPU	**1 min 9s**

Figure 5.5: Detection performance on the INRIA Person test set.

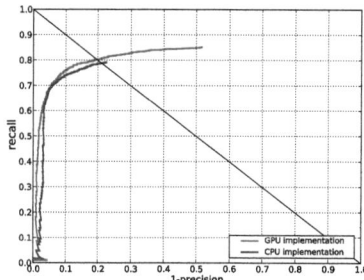

Implementation	WALL time
Our CPU	150 min 25s
Our GPU	**7 min 1s**

Figure 5.6: Detection performance on the TUDDS test set.

The TUD Dynamic Scenes dataset (TUDDS) contains 1492 cars from frontal and rear views as positive training instances. 178 full size images are available for sampling negative instances. The test dataset contains 968 images at a resolution of 752×480 pixels recorded from a driving car on highways with a total of 2007 car instances. Figure 5.4 shows some sample images.

5.6.2 Detection performance

Even though we have done our best to implement the original algorithm as close as possible, due to restructuring the algorithm and using different precision for computations, small changes in recognition performance are expected. For this reason, our first set of experiments compares our detection performance to CPU implementations in terms of recall and precision. Figure 5.5 (left) shows three curves for INRIA Person. The black curve corresponds to results obtained by running the publicly available binary written by the original author; the blue curve, performing similar to the black, is our CPU based reimplementation of Dalal and Triggs (2005); the red curve is our GPU implementation, which obtains slightly better results.

Table 5.2: Overview on detector parameters for pedestrian and car detection

(a) Detector settings for pedestrian detection

Parameter	Value
Extra Boundary	2
Blur Kernel Width	2
Window size	64 × 128
Block size	2 × 2
Cell size	8 × 8
Hor. Overlap	8
Vert. Overlap	8
Histogram Bins	9
Histogram Range	π
Gaussian Window sigma	8
Gamma Compression	Yes
Normalization	L_2-Hys
Norm. Clipping Thres.	0.2
Norm. Epsilon	1.0
Norm. Epsilon Hys	0.1
Feature vector length	3780

(b) Detector settings for car detection

Parameter	Value
Extra Boundary	0
Blur Kernel Width	N/A
Window size	20 × 20
Block size	2 × 2
Cell size	4 × 4
Hor. Overlap	4
Vert. Overlap	4
Histogram Bins	18
Histogram Range	2π
Gaussian Window Sigma	4
Gamma Compression	No
Normalization	L_1-sqrt
Norm. Clipping Thres.	0.2
Norm. Epsilon	1.0
Norm. Epsilon Hys	N/A
Feature vector length	1152

Similar findings are obtained for the experiments on the TUDDS dataset (cf. Figure 5.6). Again our GPU implementation (red curve) slightly outperforms the CPU implementation (blue curve). The improvement probably comes from floating point precision on interpolated histogram computation, since the CPU implementations use integers with rounding errors at several points, presumably for speed-ups.

5.6.3 Runtime analysis

We continue to analyze our implementation's runtime in more detail. Figure 5.5 (right) and Figure 5.6 (right) report the total runtimes[11] for the tests. On INRIA Person our implementation runs 34 times faster than Dalal's binary, and 30 times faster than our CPU reimplementation. On TUDDS our GPU implementation runs 21 times faster than our CPU implementation. Please note that these timings include I/O operations to load images from the hard disc. For most applications, however, images are directly grabbed from the camera and the overhead for loading can be neglected.

To get a better assessment of the achieved speed-up we continue to analyze the runtime of the single processing steps. Table 5.3 and Table 5.4 list the kernel runtimes and speed-ups without image acquisition on a 640 × 480 input image.

We observe a speed-up of 83 times for people detection and a speed-up by 53 times

---

[11]WALL times always indicate total running time, i.e., the "real" time reported by the `time` utility on the binary. All runtimes are measured on a Intel Core 2 Duo E6400 CPU running at 2.13GHz with 4GB of RAM.

Processing step / Implementation	CPU	GPU	Speed-up
Padding	52.5ms	1.19ms	44.1
Gradient Computation	2015.5ms	20.71ms	97.3
Histogram Computation	3359.5ms	24.44ms	137.4
Normalization	34.0ms	5.67ms	6.0
SVM evaluation	1187.9ms	27.15ms	43.7
Image Scaling	105.5ms	2.47ms	42.7
Total	6754.9ms	81.63ms	82.7

Table 5.3: Comparison of CPU and GPU runtimes for people detection for different steps of the algorithm (resolution 640 × 480, scale step 1.05)

Processing step / Implementation	CPU	GPU	Speed-up
Padding	– ms	– ms	–
Gradient Computation	717.6ms	21.01ms	34.2
Histogram Computation	3339.4ms	51.61ms	64.7
Normalization	267.5ms	10.12ms	26.4
SVM evaluation	2229.4ms	39.54ms	56.4
Image Scaling	117.1ms	2.29ms	51.2
Total	6671.0ms	124.57ms	53.6

Table 5.4: Comparison of CPU and GPU runtimes for car detection for different steps of the algorithm (resolution 640 × 480, scale step 1.05)

for the car detection experiment. In particular, gradient computation and histogram computation achieve a high speed-up for the people detector. For the car detector SVM evaluation and histogram computation have the largest speed-up. The difference of speed-ups can be explained by the different parameter settings (cf. Table 5.2) which are necessary for best detection performance. Settings of the car detector result in a less optimal hardware allocation and memory access pattern and consequently speed-up drops. Moreover, it should be noted that more windows and scales need to be scanned due to the much smaller window size.

The fact that gradient computation needs more than twice the time on the CPU but about the same time on the GPU for the pedestrian detector compared to the car detector needs further explanation. On the TUDDS car detection dataset we do not employ gamma compression. This operation would involve the computation of a square root. A more detailed analysis shows that the *sqrt()*-function consumes about half of the time on the CPU, but is optimized on the GPU due to its frequent use in computer graphics. Thus, we conclude that gamma compression which involves the *sqrt()*-function is a very expansive operation on the CPU while on the GPU it comes almost for free and might explain this difference in runtime on the CPU.

How can we make our detector even faster? First, one can try to improve the performance by reducing the overhead, e.g., by transferring more images at a time to the GPU, or by reducing kernel calls. Employing several GPUs at a time allows pipelining and the expected throughput can be further increased up to 4 times with

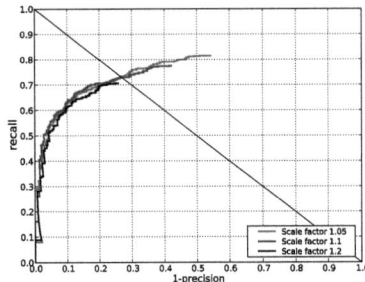

WALL times (per image)			
Downscale Factor	320× 240	640× 480	1280× 960
1.05	20ms	82ms	334ms
1.1	11ms	44ms	182ms
1.2	6ms	26ms	105ms

Figure 5.7: Increasing downscale factor on the INRIA person test set.

currently available GPU configurations. If we are ready to trade our performance for speed, small modification on the parameters may also be sufficient. Figure 5.7 shows an example, when the algorithm uses a coarser scale-space than before. Speed results are reported in a more intuitive way, on a per image basis. The experiment shows, that a small adjustment of the scale factor does not influence the precision of our detector, but causes a small drop in recall. On average, on a 320 × 240 image the localization speeds up from 49 fps to 156 fps, i.e., by a factor of 3.2.

5.7 Conclusion

In this chapter we have shown a parallel implementation of an object class detector using HOG features. For people detection our implementation runs 49 fps on 320 × 240 images, and is approximately 83 times faster than a previous CPU implementation, without any trade-off in performance. Our experiments used one single GPU only, but due to the flexible programming model, it scales up to multi-GPU systems, such as the Tesla Computing Systems with an additional expected speed-up of 2 to 4. We have also analyzed the overhead created mainly by data transfers and system calls, which defines the current limitation of these architectures.

Experiments on adjusting sliding window parameters have shown the trade-off between classification performance and speed: we have shown a detector that runs at 156 fps with similar precision, but a small drop in recall.

In the future, we plan to further improve our current implementation by reducing kernel launches and test on multi-GPU systems, as well as to adopt other features and classifiers to GPU-based architectures.

6

DYNAMIC CRFS FOR SCENE SEGMENTATION

Contents

6.1	Introduction		85
6.2	Conditional random field models		86
	6.2.1	Plain CRF: Single layer CRF model for scene-class labeling	87
	6.2.2	Object CRF: Two layer object CRF for joint object and scene labeling	87
	6.2.3	Dynamic CRF: Dynamic two layer CRF for object and scene class labeling	89
	6.2.4	Inference and parameter estimation	90
6.3	Experiments		91
	6.3.1	Features for scene labeling	91
	6.3.2	Results	93
6.4	Conclusion		98

THE previous chapters studied the detection of objects from local evidence, i.e., from features that are computed within a local window which is slid across the entire image at multiple scales. This chapter will not only model the appearance of a single object class, but also the remaining scene. It aims to understand the observed 2D scene by labeling each single pixel with its object or scene class.

As evidence gathered locally from a 2D image patch contains only limited information, we adopt the conditional random field framework (CRF) to model local neighborhood relations. However for modeling objects, the standard CRF approach is limited because of its disabilities to model long range interactions and its missing notion of object scale. We facilitate these interactions by introducing additional nodes which are instantiated from object detections (cf. Chapters 3-5). Moreover, we employ dynamic CRFs (McCallum *et al.*, 2003) to address highly dynamic scenes. A careful model design allows to handle scenes with substantially different dynamics of objects and the scene background. We evaluate our work on a challenging real-world dataset, which is recorded from an onboard camera of a driving car. Our experiments show improvements for the labeling of scene as well as object classes.

6.1 INTRODUCTION

Today, object class detection methods are capable of achieving impressive results on challenging datasets (e.g., PASCAL challenges Everingham *et al.*, 2010). Often these methods combine powerful feature vectors such as SIFT or HOG with the power of discriminant classifiers such as SVMs or AdaBoost. At the same time several authors have argued that global scene context (Torralba, 2003; Hoiem et al., 2008b) is a valuable cue for object detection and therefore should be used to support object detection. However, context-related work has nearly exclusively dealt with static scenes. This chapter specifically deals with highly dynamic scenes and will also model object motion as an additional and important cue.

Pixel-wise scene labeling has also been an active field of research recently. A common approach is to use Markov or conditional random field (CRF) models to improve performance by modeling neighborhood dependencies. Several authors have introduced the implicit notion of objects into CRF-models (e.g., He et al., 2004; Torralba et al., 2005; Kumar and Hebert, 2005; Shotton et al., 2006; Larlus et al., 2010). The interactions between object nodes and scene labels however are often limited to uni-directional information flow and therefore these models have not yet shown the full potential of simultaneously reasoning about objects and scene. By formulating the problem as a *joint* labeling problem for object and scene classes, this chapter introduces a more general notion of object-scene interaction enabling bidirectional information flow. Furthermore, as we are interested in dynamic scenes, we make use of the notion of dynamic CRFs (McCallum et al., 2003), which we extend to deal with both moving camera and moving objects.

Therefore we propose a novel approach to jointly label objects and scene classes in highly dynamic scenes for which we introduce a new real-world dataset with pixel-wise annotations. Highly dynamic scenes are not only a scientific challenge but also an important problem, e.g., for applications such as autonomous driving or video indexing where both the camera and the objects are moving independently. Formulating the problem as a joint labeling problem allows 1) to model the dynamics of the scene and the objects separately which is of particular importance for the scenario of independently moving objects and camera, and 2) to enable bi-directional information flow between object and scene class labels.

The remainder of this chapter is structured as follows. Section 6.2 introduces our approach and discusses how object detection and scene labeling can be integrated as a joint labeling problem in a dynamic CRF formulation. Section 6.3 introduces the employed features, gives details on the experiments and shows experimental results. Finally, Section 6.4 draws conclusions.

6.2 CONDITIONAL RANDOM FIELD MODELS

The following section successively introduces our model. It is divided into three parts: the first reviews single layer CRFs, the second additionally models objects in a separate layer and the last adds the scene's and objects' dynamics.

We denote the input image at time t with $\mathbf{x}^t$, the corresponding class labels at the grid cell level with $\mathbf{y}^t$ and the object labels with $\mathbf{o}^t$.

6.2.1 Plain CRF: Single layer CRF model for scene-class labeling

In general, a CRF models the conditional probability of all class labels $\mathbf{y}^t$ given an input image $\mathbf{x}^t$. Similar to others, we model the set of neighborhood relationships N_1 up to pairwise cliques to keep inference computationally tractable. Thus, we model

$$\log(P_{pCRF}(\mathbf{y}^t|\mathbf{x}^t, N_1, \Theta)) = \sum_i \Phi(y_i^t, \mathbf{x}^t; \Theta_\Phi) + \sum_{(i,j)\in N_1} \Psi(y_i^t, y_j^t, \mathbf{x}^t; \Theta_\Psi) - \log(Z^t) \tag{6.1}$$

Z^t denotes the so called partition function, which is used for normalization. N_1 is the set of all spatial pairwise neighborhoods. We refer to this model as *plain CRF*.

Unary potentials

Our unary potentials model local features for all classes C including scene as well as object classes. We employ the joint boosting framework (Torralba et al., 2007) to build a strong classifier $H(c, \mathbf{f}(x_i^t); \Theta_\Phi) = \sum_{m=1}^M h_m(c, \mathbf{f}(x_i^t); \Theta_\Phi)$. Here, $\mathbf{f}(x_i^t)$ denotes the features extracted from the input image for grid point i. M is the number of boosting rounds and c are the class labels. h_m are *weak learners* with parameters Θ_Φ and are shared among the classes for this approach. In order to interpret the boosting confidence as a probability we apply a softmax transform (Kumar and Hebert, 2005). Thus, the potential becomes:

$$\Phi(y_i^t = k, \mathbf{x}^t; \Theta_\Phi) = \log \frac{\exp H(k, \mathbf{f}(x_i^t); \Theta_\Phi)}{\sum_c \exp H(c, \mathbf{f}(x_i^t); \Theta_\Phi)} \tag{6.2}$$

Edge potentials

The edge potentials model the interaction between class labels at two neighboring sites y_i^t and y_j^t in a regular lattice. The interaction strength is modeled by a linear discriminative classifier with parameters $\Theta_\Psi = \mathbf{w}^T$ and depends on the difference of the node features $\mathbf{d}_{ij}^t := |\mathbf{f}(x_i^t) - \mathbf{f}(x_j^t)|$.

$$\Psi(y_i^t, y_j^t, \mathbf{x}^t; \Theta_\Psi) = \sum_{(k,l)\in C} \mathbf{w}^T \begin{pmatrix} 1 \\ \mathbf{d}_{ij}^t \end{pmatrix} \delta(y_i^t = k)\delta(y_j^t = l) \tag{6.3}$$

6.2.2 Object CRF: Two layer object CRF for joint object and scene labeling

Information that can be extracted from an image patch locally is rather limited and pairwise edge potentials are too weak to model long range interactions. Ideally, a complete dense layer of hidden variables would be added to encode possible locations and scales of objects, but since inference for such a model is computationally expensive we propose to inject single hidden variables $\mathbf{o}^t = \{o_1^t, \ldots, o_D^t\}$ (D being the number of detections) as depicted in Figure 6.2(a). To instantiate those nodes any multi-scale object detector can be employed.

The additional nodes draw object appearance from a strong spatial model and are connected to the set of all corresponding hidden variables $\{\mathbf{y}^t\}_{o_n^t}$ whose evidence $\{\mathbf{x}^t\}_{o_n^t}$ support the object hypotheses. The new nodes' labels in this chapter are comprised of $O = \{object, background\}$; but the extension to multiple object classes is straight forward. Thus, we introduce two new potentials into the CRF model given in (6.1) and yield the *object CRF*:

$$\log(P_{oCRF}(\mathbf{y}^t, \mathbf{o}^t | \mathbf{x}^t, \Theta)) = \log(P_{pCRF}(\mathbf{y}^t | \mathbf{x}^t, N_2, \Theta)) + \qquad (6.4)$$
$$\sum_n \Omega(o_n^t, \mathbf{x}^t; \Theta_\Omega) + \sum_{(i,j,n) \in N_3} \Lambda(y_i^t, y_j^t, o_n^t, \mathbf{x}^t; \Theta_\Psi)$$

Note that $N_2 \subset N_1$ denotes all neighborhoods where no object is present in the scene, whereas N_3 are all inter-layer neighborhoods with hypothesized object locations. Ω is the new unary object potential, whereas Λ is the inter-layer edge potential.

Unary object potentials

To define object potentials we use a state-of-the-art object detector. More specifically, we use a sliding window based multi-scale approach (cf. Chapters 3-5, Dalal and Triggs, 2005) where a window's features are defined by $\mathbf{g}(\{\mathbf{x}^t\}_{o_n^t})$ and classified with a linear SVM, the weights being $\mathbf{v}$ and b being the hyperplane's bias. To get a probabilistic interpretation for the classification margin, we adopt Platt's method (2000) and fit a sigmoid with parameters s_1 and s_2 using cross validation.

$$\Omega(o_n^t, \mathbf{x}^t; \Theta_\Omega) = \log \frac{1}{1 + \exp(s_1 \cdot (\mathbf{v}^T \cdot \mathbf{g}(\{\mathbf{x}^t\}_{o_n^t}) + b) + s_2)} \qquad (6.5)$$

Consequently, the parameters are determined as $\Theta_\Omega = \{\mathbf{v}, b, s_1, s_2\}$.

Inter-layer edge potentials

For the inter-layer edge potentials we model the neighborhood relations in cliques consisting of two underlying first layer nodes y_i^t, y_j^t and the object hypothesis node o_n^t. Similar to the pairwise edge potentials on the lower layer, the node's interaction strength is modeled by a linear classifier with weights $\Theta_\Lambda = \mathbf{u}$.

$$\Lambda(y_i^t, y_j^t, o_n^t, \mathbf{x}^t; \Theta_\Lambda) = \sum_{(k,l) \in C; m \in O} \mathbf{u}^T \begin{pmatrix} 1 \\ \mathbf{d}_{ij}^t \end{pmatrix} \delta(y_i^t = k)\delta(y_j^t = l)\delta(o_n^t = m) \qquad (6.6)$$

It is important to note, that the inter-layer interactions are anisotropic and scale-dependent. We exploit the scale given by the object detector to train different weights for different scales and thus can achieve real multi-scale modeling in the CRF framework. Furthermore, we use different sets of weights for different parts of the detected object enforcing an object and context consistent layout (Winn and Shotton, 2006).

6.2 CONDITIONAL RANDOM FIELD MODELS

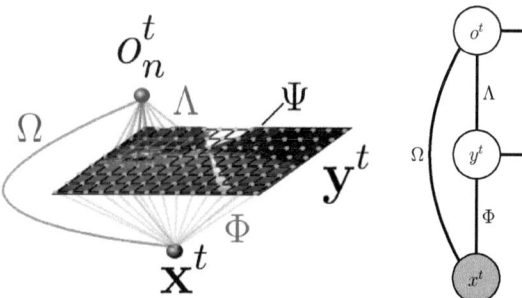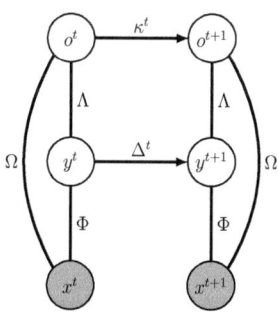

(a) Graphical model for the *object CRF*; note that different edge colors denote different potentials

(b) Graphical model for our full *dynamic CRF*; observed nodes are grey, hidden variables are white, for the sake of readability we omit the spatial layout of $\mathbf{y}^t$ with the corresponding edge potential Ψ

Figure 6.1: Graphical models for *object CRF* and *dynamic CRF*

6.2.3 Dynamic CRF: Dynamic two layer CRF for object and scene class labeling

While the additional information from an object detector already improves the classification accuracy, temporal information is a further important cue. We propose two temporal extensions to the framework introduced so far. For highly dynamic scenes – such as the image sequences taken by a driving car, which we will use as an example application to our model, it is important to note that objects and the remaining scene have different dynamics and thus should be modeled differently. For objects we estimate their motion and track them with a temporal filter in 3D space. The dynamics for the remaining scene is mainly caused by the camera motion in our example scenario. Therefore, we use an estimate of the camera's ego-motion to propagate the inferred scene labels at time t as a prior to time step $t+1$.

Since both – object and scene dynamics – transfer information forward to future time steps, we employ directed links in the corresponding graphical model as depicted in Figure 6.2(b). It would have also been possible to introduce undirected links, but those are computationally more demanding. Moreover, due to the backward flow of information in time, those might not be desirable from an application point of view when online processing is required.

Object dynamics model

In order to model the object dynamics we employ multiple extended Kalman filters (Kalman, 1960) – one for each object. For the dynamic scenes dataset, which we will use for the experimental section, the camera calibration is known and the sequences are recorded from a driving car. Additionally, we assume the objects to stand on the ground plane. Consequently, extended Kalman filters (EKFs) are able to model the object position in 3D coordinates. Additionally, the state vector contains the objects' width and speed on the ground plane as well as the camera's tilt and all state variables' first derivative with respect to time.

For the motion model we employ linear motion dynamics with the acceleration being modeled as system noise which proved sufficient for the image sequences used below. The tracks' confidences are given by the last associated detection's score. Hence, we obtain the following integrated model:

$$\log(P_{tCRF}(\mathbf{y}^t, \mathbf{o}^t | \mathbf{x}^t, \Theta)) = \log(P_{pCRF}(\mathbf{y}^t | \mathbf{x}^t, N_2, \Theta)) + \qquad (6.7)$$
$$\sum_n \kappa^t(o_n^t, \mathbf{o}^{t-1}, \mathbf{x}^t; \Theta_\kappa) + \sum_{(i,j,n) \in N_3} \Lambda(y_i^t, y_j^t, o_n^t, \mathbf{x}^t; \Theta_\Lambda)$$

where κ^t models the probability of an object hypothesis o_n^t at time t given the history of input images. It replaces the previously introduced potentials for objects Ω. The parameter vector consists of the detector's parameters and additionally of the Kalman filter's dynamics $\{A, W\}$ and measurement model $\{H_t, V_t\}$ and thus $\Theta_\kappa = \Theta_\Omega \cup \{A, W, H_t, V_t\}$.

Scene dynamic model

In the spirit of recursive Bayesian state estimation under the Markovian assumption, the posterior distribution of $\mathbf{y}^{t-1}$ is used as a prior to time step t. However, for dynamic scenes the image content needs to be transformed to associate the grid points with the right posterior distributions. In this chapter we estimate the projection Q from $\mathbf{y}^t$ to $\mathbf{y}^{t+1}$ given the camera's translation and calibration (Θ_{Δ^t}). Thus, we obtain an additional unary potential for $\mathbf{y}^t$.

$$\Delta^t(y_i^t, \mathbf{y}^{t-1}; \Theta_{\Delta^t}) = \log(P_{tCRF}(y_{Q^{-1}(i)}^{t-1} | \Theta)) \qquad (6.8)$$

The complete *dynamic CRF* model including both object and scene dynamics as depicted in Figure 6.2(b) then is

$$\log(P_{dCRF}(\mathbf{y}^t, \mathbf{o}^t, \mathbf{x}^t | \mathbf{y}^{t-1}, \mathbf{o}^{t-1}, \Theta)) = \log(P_{tCRF}(\mathbf{y}^t, \mathbf{o}^t | \mathbf{x}^t, \Theta)) + \qquad (6.9)$$
$$\sum_i \Delta^t(y_i^t, \mathbf{y}^{t-1}; \Theta_{\Delta^t})$$

6.2.4 Inference and parameter estimation

For inference in the undirected graphical models we employ sum-product loopy belief propagation with a parallel message update schedule. For parameter estimation we take a piecewise learning approach (Sutton and McCallum, 2005) by assuming the parameters of unary potentials to be conditionally independent of the edge potentials' parameters.

While this no longer guarantees to find the optimal parameter setting for Θ, we can learn the model much faster as discussed by Sutton and McCallum (2005).

Thus, prior to learning the edge potential models we train parameters Θ_Φ, Θ_Ω for the unary potentials. The parameter set Θ_κ for the Kalman filter is set to reasonable values by hand.

Finally, the edge potentials' parameter sets Θ_Ψ and Θ_Λ are learned jointly in a maximum likelihood setting with stochastic meta descent. As proposed by Vishwanathan et al. (2006) we assume a Gaussian prior with meta parameter σ on the linear weights to avoid overfitting. The according gradients are determined as:

$$\frac{\partial \mathcal{L}(\Theta)}{\partial \Theta_\Psi} = \frac{\Theta_\Psi}{\sigma^2} - \sum_{(i,j)\in N_2} \sum_{(k,l)\in C} (\delta(y_i^t = k)\delta(y_j^t = l) -$$
$$\langle \delta(y_i^t = k)\delta(y_j^t = l) \rangle) \begin{pmatrix} 1 \\ \mathbf{d}_{ij}^t \end{pmatrix} \qquad (6.10)$$

$$\frac{\partial \mathcal{L}(\Theta)}{\partial \Theta_\Lambda} = \frac{\Theta_\Lambda}{\sigma^2} - \sum_{(i,j,n)\in N_3} \sum_{(k,l)\in C, m\in O} (\delta(y_i^t = k)\delta(y_j^t = l)\delta(o_n^t = m) -$$
$$\langle \delta(y_i^t = k)\delta(y_j^t = l)\delta(o_n^t = m) \rangle) \begin{pmatrix} 1 \\ \mathbf{d}_{ij}^t \end{pmatrix} \qquad (6.11)$$

$\mathcal{L}(\Theta)$ is the likelihood of observing the training data given the model parameters Θ. The expectation $\langle \cdot \rangle$ is approximated by the pseudo-marginals returned by loopy belief propagation since exact computation is intractable.

6.3 EXPERIMENTS

To evaluate our model's performance we conducted several experiments on two datasets. First, we describe our features which are used for texture and location based classification of scene labels on the scene label CRF layer. Then we introduce features employed for object detection on the object label CRF layer. Next, we briefly discuss the results obtained on the Sowerby database and finally we present results on image sequences on a new dynamic scenes dataset, which consist of car traffic image sequences recorded from a driving vehicle under challenging real-world conditions.

6.3.1 Features for scene labeling

Texture and location features

For the unary potential Φ at the lower level as well as for the edge potentials Ψ and inter-layer potentials Λ we employ texture and location features. The texture features are computed from the 16 first coefficients of the Walsh-Hadamard transform. Figure 6.4(a) visualizes the used transformation kernels. This transformation is a discrete approximation of the cosine transform and can be computed efficiently (Hel-Or and

Figure 6.2: We employ a gray world assumption to normalize input images. The first image row shows unnormalized images, while the second shows the normalized results. Note that normalization yields more homogeneous images with respect to color and illumination and thus facilitates the use of texture features under challenging real-world conditions.

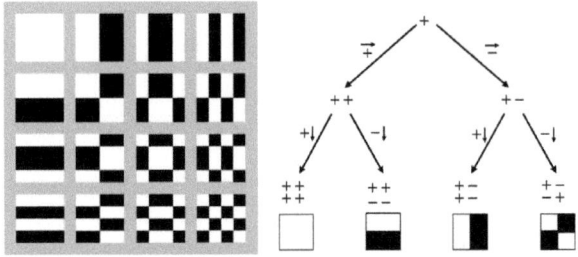

(a) First 16 filter kernels of the Walsh-Hadamard transform

(b) The Walsh-Hadamard transform can be computed efficiently by exploiting a tree structure (Hel-Or and Hel-Or, 2005)

Figure 6.3: First Walsh-Hadamard filterbank kernels and its efficient computation

Hel-Or, 2005; Alon et al., 2006) – even in real-time (e.g., on modern graphics hardware) by exploiting a tree scheme (cf. Figure 6.4(b)).

The features are extracted at multiple scales from all channels of the input image in CIE *Lab* color space. As a preprocessing step, a and b channels are normalized by means of a gray world assumption to cope with varying color appearance. The L channel is mean-variance normalized to fit a Gaussian distribution with a fixed mean to cope with global lighting variations. See Figure 6.2 for a comparison of normalized to unnormalized images. We also found that normalizing the transformation's coefficients according to Varma and Zisserman (2002) is beneficial. They propose to L_1-normalize each filter response first and then locally normalize the responses at each image pixel. Finally, we take the mean and variance of the normalized responses as feature for each node in the regular CRF lattice. Additionally, we use the grid point's coordinates within the image as a location cue. Therefore, we concatenate the pixel coordinates to the feature vector.

6.3 EXPERIMENTS

	Pixel-wise accuracy	
	Unary classification	plain CRF model
He et al. (2004)	82.4%	89.5%
Kumar and Hebert (2005)	85.4%	89.3%
Shotton et al. (2006)	**85.6%**	88.6%
Our approach	84.5%	**91.1%**

Table 6.1: Comparison to previously reported results on the Sowerby dataset

HOG

In the experiments described below we employ a HOG (Histogram of Oriented Gradients) detector (Dalal and Triggs, 2005) to generate object hypotheses. This is a sliding window approach where features are computed on a dense grid. First, histograms of gradient orientation are computed in *cells* performing interpolation with respect to the gradient's location and with respect to the magnitude. Next, sets of neighboring cells are grouped into overlapping *blocks*, which are normalized to achieve invariance to different illumination conditions. Our front and rear view car detector has a window size of 20 × 20 pixels. It is trained on a separate dataset of front and rear car views containing 1492 positive instances from the LabelMe database (Russell et al., 2008) and 178 negative images.

6.3.2 Results

Sowerby dataset

The Sowerby dataset is a widely used benchmark for CRFs, which contains 7 outdoor rural landscape classes. The dataset comprises 104 images at a resolution of 96 × 64 pixels. Following the protocol of Kumar and Hebert (2005) we randomly selected 60 images for training and 44 images for testing. Some example images with inferred labels are shown in Figure 6.4. However, this dataset does neither contain image sequences nor cars that can be detected with an object detector and thus we can only compare our *plain CRF* model (Equation (6.1)) with previous work on this set.

The experiments show that our features and CRF parameter estimation is competitive to other state-of-the-art methods. Table 6.1 gives an overview of previously published results and how those compare to our model (see Figure 6.5). While the more sophisticated Textons features (Shotton et al., 2006) do better for unary classification, our CRF model can outperform those since our edge potentials are learned from training data. For this dataset we use a grid with one node for each input pixel, while the Gaussian prior σ was set to 1.25. The Walsh-Hadamard transform was run on the input images at the aperture size of 2, 4, 8 and 16 pixels. Moreover, we used a global set of weights for the linear classifiers of the edge potentials, but distinguish between north-south neighborhood relations and east-west neighborhood relations.

Figure 6.4: *Sowerby* dataset example results

Dynamic scenes dataset

To evaluate our *object* and *dynamic CRF* we set up a new *dynamic scenes* dataset with image sequences consisting of overall 1936 images[12]. The images are taken from a camera inside a driving car and mainly show highways with high dynamics of driving vehicles at an image resolution of 752 × 480 pixels. Cars appear at all scales from as small as 15 pixels up to 200 pixels. The database consists of 176 sequences with 11 successive images each. It is split into equal size training and test sets of 968 images.

To evaluate pixel level labeling accuracy the last frame of each sequence is labeled pixel-wise, while the remainder only contains bounding box annotations for the frontal and rear view car object class. Overall, the dataset contains the eight labels *void*, *sky*, *road*, *lane marking*, *building*, *trees & bushes*, *grass* and *car*. Figure 6.5 shows some sample scenes. For the following experiments we used 8 × 8 pixels for each CRF grid node and texture features were extracted at the aperture sizes of 8, 16 and 32 pixels.

We start with an evaluation of the unary classifier performance on the scene class layer. Table 6.2 lists the pixel-wise classification accuracy for different variations of the feature. As expected location is a valuable cue, since there is a huge variation in appearance due to different lighting conditions. Those range from bright and sunny illumination with cast shadows to overcast. Additionally, motion blur and weak contrast complicate the pure appearance-based classification. Further, we observe that normalization (Varma and Zisserman, 2002) as well as multi-scale features are helpful to improve the classification results.

Next, we analyze the performance of the different proposed CRF models. On the one hand we report the overall pixel-wise accuracy. On the other hand the pixel-wise labeling performance on the car object class is of particular interest. Overall, car pixels cover 1.3% of the overall observed pixels. Yet, those are an important fraction for many applications and thus we also report those for our evaluation.

For the experiments we used pixel location dependent linear edge potential classifiers

---

[12]The dataset is available at http://www.mis.informatik.tu-darmstadt.de.

6.3 EXPERIMENTS

		Normalization			
		on		off	
		multi-scale	single-scale	multi-scale	single-scale
Location	on	**82.2%**	81.1%	79.7%	79.7%
	off	69.1%	64.1%	62.3%	62.3%

Table 6.2: Evaluation of texture location features based on overall pixel-wise accuracy; Multi-scale includes feature scales of 8, 16 and 32 pixels, Single-scale is a feature scale of 8 pixels; note that these number do not include the CRF model – adding the *plain CRF* to the best configuration yields an overall accuracy of 88.3%.

	Plain CRF (No object layer)			Object CRF (With object layer)			Including EKF object dynamics		
	Recall	Prec.	Acc.	Recall	Prec.	Acc.	Recall	Prec.	Acc.
CRF	50.1%	57.7%	88.3%	62.9%	52.3%	88.6%	70.4%	57.8%	88.7%
dyn. CRF	25.5%	44.8%	86.5%	75.7%	50.8%	87.1%	78.0%	51.0%	88.1%

Table 6.3: Pixel-wise recall and precision for the pixels labeled as *car* and overall accuracy on all classes. First row reports performance without the posterior's temporal propagation (cf. Section 6.2.3); second row includes temporal propagation.

with 16 parameter sets, arranged in four rows and four columns. Moreover, we distinguish between north-south and east-west neighborhoods. For the inter-layer edge potentials we trained different weight sets depending on detection scale (discretized in 6 bins) and depending on the neighborhood location with respect to the object's center.

Table 6.3 shows recall and precision for the proposed models. Firstly, the employed detector has an equal error rate of 78.8% when the car detections are evaluated in terms of precision and recall. When evaluated on a pixel-wise basis the performance corresponds to 60.2% recall. The missing 39.8% are mostly due to the challenging dataset. It contains cars with weak contrast, cars at small scales and partially visible cars leaving the field of view. Precision for the detector evaluated on pixels is 37.7%. Wrongly classified pixels are mainly around the objects and on structured background on which the detector obtains false detections.

Let us now turn to the performance of the different CRF models. Without higher level information from an object detector *plain CRFs* in combination with texture-location features achieve a recall of 50.1% with a precision of 57.7%. The recognition of cars in this setup is problematic since CRFs optimize a global energy function, while the car class only constitutes a minor fraction of the data. Thus, the result is mainly dominated by classes which occupy the largest regions such as sky, road and trees.

With higher level object information (*object CRF*) recall can be improved up to 62.9% with slightly lower precision resulting from the detector's false positive detections. However, when objects are additionally tracked with a Kalman filter, we achieve a recall of 70.4% with a precision of 57.8%. This proves that the object labeling for the car object class leverages from the object detector and additionally from the dynamic

True class	Data fraction	Inferred	Sky	Road	Lane marking	Trees & bushes	Grass	Building	Void	Car
Sky	10.4%	**91.0**	0.0	0.0	7.7	0.5	0.4	0.3	0.1
Road	42.1%	0.0	**95.7**	1.0	0.3	1.1	0.1	0.5	1.3
Lane marking	1.9%	0.0	36.3	**56.4**	0.8	2.9	0.2	1.8	1.6
Trees & bushes	29.2%	1.5	0.2	0.0	**91.5**	5.0	0.2	1.1	0.4
Grass	12.1%	0.4	5.7	0.5	13.4	**75.3**	0.3	3.5	0.9
Building	0.3%	1.6	0.2	0.1	37.8	4.4	**48.4**	6.3	1.2
Void	2.7%	6.4	15.9	4.1	27.7	29.1	1.4	**10.6**	4.8
Car	1.3%	0.3	3.9	0.2	8.2	4.9	2.1	2.4	**78.0**

Table 6.4: Confusion matrix in percent for the *dynamic scenes* dataset; entries are row-normalized

modeling by a Kalman filter.

Additionally, we observe an improvement of the overall labeling accuracy. While *plain CRFs* obtain an accuracy of 88.3%, the *object CRF* achieves 88.6% while also including object dynamics further improves the overall labeling accuracy to 88.7%. The relative number of 0.4% might appear low, but considering that the database overall only has 1.3% car pixels, this is worth noting. Thus, we conclude that not only the labeling on the car class is improved but also the overall scene labeling quality.

When the scene dynamics are modeled additionally and posteriors are propagated over time (*dynamic CRF*), we again observe an improvement of the achieved recall from 25.5% to 75.7% with the additional object nodes. And also the objects' dynamic model can further improve the recall to 78.0% correctly labeled pixels. Thus, again we can conclude that the CRF model exploits both the information given by the object detector as well as the additional object dynamic to improve the labeling quality.

Finally, when the overall accuracy is analyzed while the scene dynamic is modeled we observe a minor drop compared to the static modeling. However, we again consistently observe that the object information and their dynamics allow to improve from 86.5% without object information to 87.1% with *object CRFs* and to 88.1% with the full model.

The consistently slightly worse precision and overall accuracy for the dynamic scene models need to be explained. Non-car pixels wrongly labeled as car are mainly located at the object boundary, which are mainly due to artifacts of the scene label forward propagation. Those are introduced by the inaccuracies of the speedometer and due to the inaccuracies of the projection estimation. In the future, leveraging optic flow estimates might be a promising way to associate pixels more accurately over time.

A confusion matrix for all classes of the *dynamic scenes* database can be found in Table 6.4. Figure 6.5 shows sample detections and scene labelings for the different CRF models to illustrate the impact of the different models and their improvements. In example (d) for instance the car which is leaving the field of view is mostly smoothed out by a *plain CRF* and *object CRF*, while the *dynamic CRF* is able to classify almost

6.3 EXPERIMENTS

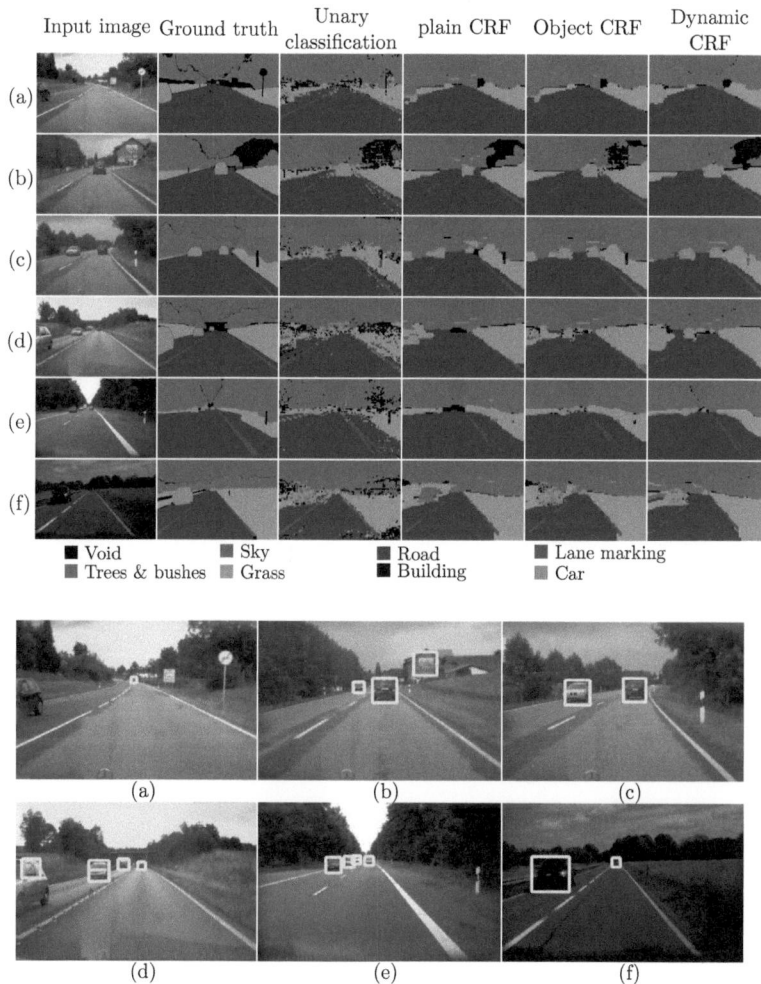

Figure 6.5: *Dynamic scenes* dataset example scene labeling results and corresponding detections in left-right order (best viewed in color); note that detections can be overruled by the texture location potentials and vice versa

the entire area correctly. Additionally, the smaller cars which get smoothed out by a *plain CRF* are classified correctly by the *object* and *dynamic CRF*. Also note that false object detections as in example (b) do not result in a wrong labeling of the scene.

6.4 CONCLUSION

In this chapter we have presented a unifying model for joint scene and object class labeling. While CRFs greatly improve unary pixel-wise classification of scenes they tend to smooth out smaller regions and objects such as cars in landscape scenes. This is particularly true when objects only comprise a minor part of the amount of overall pixels. We showed that adding higher level information from a state-of-the-art HOG object detector ameliorates this shortcoming. Further improvement – especially when objects are only partially visible – is achieved when object dynamics are properly modeled and when scene labeling information is propagated over time.

The improvement obtained is bidirectional, on the one hand the labeling of object classes is improved, but on the other hand also the remaining scene classes benefit from the additional source of information.

In Chapter 7 we will investigate how relations between different objects such as partial occlusion can be modeled when multiple object classes are detected. Additionally, we seek to improve the ego-motion estimation of the camera to further improve the performance. This will also allow us to employ motion features in the future. Finally, we assume that the integration of different sensors such as RADAR allow for a further improvement of the results.

7 MONOCULAR 3D SCENE MODELING AND INFERENCE

Contents

7.1	Introduction		**99**
7.2	Single-frame 3D scene model		**101**
	7.2.1	Inference framework	103
	7.2.2	Proposal moves	103
	7.2.3	Projective 3D to 2D marginalization	105
7.3	Multi-frame scene model and inference		**105**
	7.3.1	Multi-frame 3D scene tracklet model	105
	7.3.2	Long term data association with scene tracking	106
7.4	Datasets and implementation details		**107**
7.5	Experimental results		**109**
7.6	Conclusion		**116**

THE previous chapter studied how road scenes can be understood in 2D image space. We showed that improved segmentation performance can be achieved when object detections and bottom-up scene labels are combined in a dynamic CRF framework. However, models in 2D image space are limited when the application scenario is inherently 3D. Robots and driver assistance systems, for instance, have to react to the perceived environment and control physical processes. To achieve this the scene must be inferred in a world coordinate system.

This chapter is addressing this requirement by formulating a probabilistic 3D scene model for joint inference of 3D object positions and camera pose. As input we employ the detector framework of Chapter 4 and the scene labeling approach of Chapter 6. By exploiting the ideas of *scene tracklets*, *tracking-by-detection* and *3D scene context* we are able to robustly infer a 3D world model from a mobile observer. Our model only requires a single monocular camera and odometry information from motion sensors.

Our approach is evaluated for the three object classes *pedestrians*, *cars* and *trucks* on several challenging datasets. We consistently outperform state-of-the-art object detectors as well as standard Kalman filter tracking. For pedestrians we also outperform the stereo-camera based system by Ess *et al.* (2009a).

7.1 INTRODUCTION

Robustly tracking objects from a moving observer is an active research area due to its importance for driver assistance, traffic safety, and autonomous navigation (Ess *et al.*, 2009a; Gavrila and Munder, 2007). Dynamically changing backgrounds, varying lighting

Figure 7.1: Our system performs 3D inference to reinforce weakly detected objects and to prune false positive detections by exploiting evidence from scene labeling and an object detector. *(left)* Detector input; *(middle)* single-frame 3D inference with overlaid scene labeling and horizon estimate; *(right)* multi-frame tracking results (all results at 0.1 FPPI). See Section 7.5 for a detailed discussion.

conditions, and the low viewpoint of vehicle-mounted cameras all contribute to the difficulty of the problem. Furthermore, to support navigation, object locations should be estimated in a global 3D coordinate frame rather than in image coordinates.

The main goal of this chapter is to address this important and challenging problem by proposing a new *probabilistic 3D scene model*. Our model builds upon several important lessons from previous research: (1) robust tracking performance is currently best achieved with a *tracking-by-detection* framework (e.g., Okuma *et al.*, 2004); (2) short term evidence aggregation, typically termed *tracklets* (Kaucic *et al.*, 2005), allows for increased tracking robustness; (3) the objects should not be modeled in isolation, but in their *3D scene context*, which puts strong constraints on the position and motion of tracked objects (Hoiem *et al.*, 2008b; Ess *et al.*, 2009a); and (4) *multi-cue combination* of scene labels and object detectors allows to strengthen weak detections, but also to prune inconsistent false detections (Hoiem *et al.*, 2008b). While all these different components have been shown to boost performance individually, in the present work, for the first time, we integrate them all in a single system. As our experiments show, the proposed probabilistic 3D scene model significantly outperforms the current state-of-the-art. Figure 7.1 shows example results for two different types of challenging onboard sequences. Our system is able to robustly track a varying number of targets in 3D world coordinates in highly dynamic scenes. This enables us to use a single camera only instead of relying on stereo cameras as in previous work (e.g., Ess *et al.*, 2009a; Gavrila and Munder, 2007).

Despite using only monocular input, the proposed model allows to constrain object detections to geometrically feasible locations and enforces physically plausible 3D dynamics. This improves object detection results by pruning physically implausible

7.2 SINGLE-FRAME 3D SCENE MODEL

false positives and strengthening weak detections along an object's trajectory. We demonstrate that accumulating scene evidence over a small number of frames with help of a 3D scene model significantly improves performance. As exact inference is intractable we employ reversible-jump Markov Chain Monte Carlo (RJMCMC) sampling to approximate per-frame distributions. Further improvement can be achieved by performing long-term data association with a Hidden Markov Model (HMM).

We start by giving a detailed description of the model in Section 7.2 and Section 7.3. We then discuss implementation and experimental details (Section 7.4), and present quantitative results, and discuss the model's advantages and limitations using example results (Section 7.5). A summary and outlook conclude this chapter (Section 7.6).

7.2 SINGLE-FRAME 3D SCENE MODEL

We begin by describing our 3D scene model for a *single image*, which aims at combining available prior knowledge with image evidence in order to reconstruct the 3D positions of all objects in the scene. For clarity, the time index t is omitted when referring to a single time step only. Variables in image coordinates are printed in lower case, variables in 3D world coordinates in upper case; vectors are printed in bold face.

The posterior distribution for the 3D scene state $\mathbf{X}$ given image evidence $\mathcal{E}$ is defined in the usual way, in terms of a prior and an observation model:

$$P(\mathbf{X}|\mathcal{E}) \propto P(\mathcal{E}|\mathbf{X})P(\mathbf{X}) \qquad (7.1)$$

The 3D state $\mathbf{X}$ consists of the individual states of all objects $\mathbf{O}^i$, described by their relative 3D position $(O_x^i, O_y^i, O_z^i)^\top$ w.r.t. the observer and by their height H^i. Moreover, $\mathbf{X}$ includes the internal camera parameters $\mathbf{K}$ and the camera orientation $\mathbf{R}$.

The goal of this work is to infer the 3D state $\mathbf{X}$ from video data of a monocular, forward facing camera (see Figure 7.2). While in general this is an under-constrained problem, in robotic and automotive applications we can make the following assumptions that are expressed in the prior $P(\mathbf{X})$: The camera undergoes no roll and yaw w.r.t. the platform, its intrinsics $\mathbf{K}$ are constant and have been calibrated off-line, and the speed and turn rate of the platform are estimated from odometer readings. Furthermore, the platform as well as all objects of interest are constrained to stand on a common ground plane (i.e., $O_z^i = 0$). Note that under these assumptions the ground plane in camera-centric coordinates is fully determined by the pitch angle Θ. As the camera is rigidly mounted to the vehicle, it can only pitch a few degrees. To avoid degenerate camera configurations, the pitch angle is therefore modeled as normally distributed around the pitch of the resting platform as observed during calibration: $\mathcal{N}(\Theta; \mu_\Theta, \sigma_\Theta)$. This prior allows deviations arising from acceleration and braking of the observer. This is particularly important for the estimation of distant objects as, due to the low camera viewpoint, even minor changes in the pitch may cause a large error for distance estimation in the far field.

Moreover, we assume the height of all scene objects to follow a normal distribution around a known mean value, which is specific for the respective object class c_i,

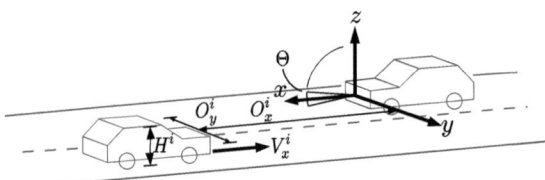

Figure 7.2: Visualization of the 3D scene state $\mathbf{X}$ in the world coordinate system. Note that the camera is mounted to the vehicle on the right.

$\mathcal{N}(H^i; \mu_H^{c_i}, \sigma_H^{c_i})$. This helps to prune false detections that are consistent with the ground plane, but are of the wrong height (e.g., background structures such as street lights). The overall prior is thus given as

$$P(\mathbf{X}) \propto \mathcal{N}(\Theta; \mu_\Theta, \sigma_\Theta) \cdot \prod_i \mathcal{N}(H^i; \mu_H^{c_i}, \sigma_H^{c_i}) \qquad (7.2)$$

Next, we turn to the observation model $P(\mathcal{E}|\mathbf{X})$. The image evidence $\mathcal{E}$ is comprised of a set of potential object detections and a scene labeling, i.e., category labels densely estimated for every pixel. As we will see in the experiments, the combination of these two types of image evidence is beneficial as object detections give reliable but rather coarse bounding boxes, and low level cues enable more fine-grained data association by penalizing inconsistent associations and supporting consistent, but weak detections.

For each object our model fuses object appearance given by the object detector confidence, geometric constraints, and local evidence from bottom-up pixel-wise labeling:

$$P(\mathcal{E}|\mathbf{X}) \propto \prod_i \Psi_D\!\left(\mathbf{d}^{a(i)}\right) \cdot \Psi_G\!\left(\mathbf{O}^i, \Theta; \mathbf{d}^{a(i)}\right) \cdot \Psi_L^i\!\left(\mathbf{X}; \mathbf{l}\right) \qquad (7.3)$$

Here, $a(i)$ denotes the association function, which assigns a candidate object detection $\mathbf{d}^{a(i)}$ to every 3D object hypothesis $\mathbf{O}^i$. Note that the associations between objects and detections are established as part of the MCMC sampling procedure (see Section 7.2.2). The appearance potential Ψ_D maps the appearance score of detection $\mathbf{d}^{a(i)}$ for object i into the positive range. Depending on the employed classifier, we use different mappings – see Section 7.4 for details.

The geometry potential Ψ_G models how well the estimated 3D state $\mathbf{O}^i$ satisfies the geometric constraints due to the ground plane specified by the camera pitch Θ. Denoting the projection of the 3D position $\mathbf{O}^i$ to the image plane as $\mathbf{o}^i$, the distance between $\mathbf{o}^i$ and the associated detection $\mathbf{d}^{a(i)}$ in x-y-scale-space serves as a measure of how much the geometric constraints are violated. We model Ψ_G using a Gaussian

$$\Psi_G(\mathbf{O}^i, \Theta; \mathbf{d}^{a(i)}) = \mathcal{N}(\mathbf{o}^i; \mathbf{d}^{a(i)}, \boldsymbol{\sigma}_G + \bar{\boldsymbol{\sigma}}_G), \qquad (7.4)$$

where we split the kernel bandwidth into a constant component $\boldsymbol{\sigma}_G$ and a scale-dependent component $\bar{\boldsymbol{\sigma}}_G$ to account for inaccuracies that arise from the scanning stride of the sliding window detectors.

7.2 SINGLE-FRAME 3D SCENE MODEL

The scene labeling potential Ψ_L^i describes how well the projection $\mathbf{o}^i$ matches the bottom-up pixel labeling. For each pixel j and each class c the labeling yields a classification score $l^j(c)$. Similar to Ψ_D, the labeling scores are normalized pixel-wise by means of a softmax transformation in order to obtain positive values.

It is important to note that this cue demands 3D scene modeling: To determine the set of pixels that belong to each potential object, one needs to account for inter-object occlusions, and hence know the objects' depth ordering (cf. Isard and MacCormick, 2001). Given that ordering, we proceed as follows: each object is back-projected to a bounding box $\mathbf{o}^i$, and that box is split into a visible region $\boldsymbol{\delta}^i$ and an occluded region $\boldsymbol{\omega}^i$. The object likelihood is then defined as the ratio between the cumulative score for the expected label e and the cumulative score of the pixel-wise best label $k \neq e$, evaluated over the visible part of $\mathbf{o}^i$:

$$\Psi_L^i(\mathbf{X};1) = \left(\frac{\sum_{j \in \boldsymbol{\delta}^i} l^j(e) + \tau}{\epsilon|\boldsymbol{\omega}^i| + \sum_{j \in \boldsymbol{\delta}^i} l^j(k) + \tau} \right)^\alpha , \qquad (7.5)$$

where the constant τ corresponds to a weak Dirichlet prior; $\epsilon|\boldsymbol{\omega}^i|$ avoids highly occluded objects to have a large influence with little available evidence; and α balances the relative importance of detector score and pixel label likelihood.

Importantly, $P(\mathbf{X}|\mathcal{E})$ is not comparable across scene configurations with different numbers of objects. We address this with a reversible jump MCMC framework (Green, 1995).

7.2.1 Inference framework

To perform inference in the above model, we simulate the posterior distribution $P(\mathbf{X}|\mathcal{E})$ in a Metropolis-Hastings MCMC framework (Gilks et al., 1995). At each iteration s new scene samples $\mathbf{X}'$ are proposed by different *moves* from the proposal density $Q(\mathbf{X}'; \mathbf{X}^{(s)})$. The proposal's posterior is evaluated and the *acceptance ratio* is computed as

$$r = \frac{P(\mathbf{X}'|\mathcal{E})}{P(\mathbf{X}^{(s)}|\mathcal{E})} \frac{Q(\mathbf{X}^{(s)}; \mathbf{X}')}{Q(\mathbf{X}'; \mathbf{X}^{(s)})}. \qquad (7.6)$$

The proposal is accepted with probability $\min(1; r)$. We assign $\mathbf{X}^{(s+1)} \leftarrow \mathbf{X}'$ if the proposal is accepted; otherwise the last state is retained, $\mathbf{X}^{(s+1)} \leftarrow \mathbf{X}^{(s)}$. Since our goal is to sample from the equilibrium distribution, we discard the samples from an initial burn-in phase. Note that the normalization of the posterior does not have to be known, since it is independent of $\mathbf{X}$ and therefore cancels out in the posterior ratio.

7.2.2 Proposal moves

Proposal moves change the current state of the Markov chain. We employ three different move types: *diffusion moves* to update the last state's variables, *add moves* and *delete moves* to change the state's dimensionality by adding or removing objects from the scene. Add and delete moves are mutually reversible and trans-dimensional. At each iteration, the move type is selected randomly with fixed probabilities $q_{\text{Add}}, q_{\text{Del}}$ and q_{Dif}.

Diffusion moves change the current state by sampling new values for the state variables. At each diffusion move, object variables are updated with a probability of q_O, while Θ is updated with a probability of q_Θ.

To update objects we draw the index i of the object to update from a uniform distribution and then update $\mathbf{O}^i$. Proposals are drawn from a multi-variate normal distribution centered at the position of the previous state and with diagonal covariance.

To update the camera pitch Θ proposals are generated from a mixture model. The first mixture component is a broad normal distribution centered at the calibrated pitch for the motionless platform. For the remaining mixture components, we assume distant objects associated with detections at small scales to have the class' mean height and use $\mathbf{d}^{a(i)}$ to compute their distance by means of the theorem of intersecting lines. Then the deviation between the detected bounding box and the object's projection in the image allows one to estimate the camera pitch. We place one mixture component around each pitch computed this way and assign mixture weights proportional to the detection scores to put more weight on more likely objects.

Add moves add a new object $\mathbf{O}^{N+1}$ to the chain's last state, where N is the number of objects contained in $\mathbf{X}^{(s)}$. As this move is trans-dimensional (i.e., the number of dimensions of $\mathbf{X}^{(s)}$ and $\mathbf{X}'$ do not match) special consideration needs to be taken when the posterior ratio $\frac{P(\mathbf{X}'|\mathcal{E})}{P(\mathbf{X}^{(s)}|\mathcal{E})}$ is evaluated. In particular, $P(\mathbf{X}^{(s)}|\mathcal{E})$ needs to be made comparable in the state space of $P(\mathbf{X}'|\mathcal{E})$. To this end, we assume a constant probability $\bar{P}(\mathbf{O}^{N+1})$ for each object to be part of the background. Hence, posteriors of states with different numbers of objects can be compared in the higher dimensional state space by transforming $P(\mathbf{X}^{(s)}|\mathcal{E})$ to

$$\hat{P}(\mathbf{X}^{(s)}|\mathcal{E}) = P(\mathbf{X}^{(s)}|\mathcal{E})\bar{P}(\mathbf{O}^{N+1}) \qquad (7.7)$$

To efficiently explore high density regions of the posterior we use the detection scores in the proposal distribution. A new object index n is drawn from the discrete set of all K detections $\{\bar{d}\}$, which are not yet associated with an object in the scene, according to $Q(\mathbf{X}';\mathbf{X}^{(s)}) = \frac{\psi_D(\bar{d}^n)}{\sum_k \psi_D(\bar{d}^k)}$. The data association function is updated by letting $a(N+1)$ associate the new object with the selected detection. For distant objects (i.e., detections at small scales) we instantiate the new object at a distance given through the theorem of intersecting lines and the height prior, whereas for objects in the near-field a more accurate 3D position can be estimated from the ground plane and camera calibration.

Delete moves remove an object $\mathbf{O}^n$ from the last state and move the associated detection $\mathbf{d}^{a(n)}$ back to $\{\bar{d}\}$. Similar to the add move, the proposed lower dimensional state $\mathbf{X}'$ needs to be transformed. The object index n to be removed from the scene is drawn uniformly among all objects currently in the scene, thus $Q(\mathbf{X}';\mathbf{X}^{(s)}) = \frac{1}{N}$.

Consequently, the acceptance ratios for add and delete moves are:

$$r_{\text{Add}} = \frac{P(\mathbf{X}'|\mathcal{E})}{\hat{P}(\mathbf{X}^{(s)}|\mathcal{E})} \frac{q_{\text{Del}}}{q_{\text{Add}}} \frac{\sum_k \psi_D(\bar{\mathbf{d}}^k)}{\psi_D(\bar{\mathbf{d}}^n)(N+1)} \tag{7.8}$$

$$r_{\text{Del}} = \frac{\hat{P}(\mathbf{X}'|\mathcal{E})}{P(\mathbf{X}^{(s)}|\mathcal{E})} \frac{q_{\text{Add}}}{q_{\text{Del}}} \frac{N\psi_D(\mathbf{d}^{a(n)})}{\psi_D(\mathbf{d}^{a(n)}) + \sum_k \psi_D(\bar{\mathbf{d}}^k)} \tag{7.9}$$

7.2.3 Projective 3D to 2D marginalization

In order to obtain a score for a 2D position $\mathbf{u}$ (including scale) from our 3D scene model, the probabilistic framework suggests marginalizing over all possible 3D scenes $\mathbf{X}$ that contain an object that projects to that 2D position:

$$P(\mathbf{u}|\mathcal{E}) = \int \max_i \left(\left[\mathbf{u} = \mathbf{o}^i\right]\right) P(\mathbf{X}|\mathcal{E}) \, \mathrm{d}\mathbf{X} \,, \tag{7.10}$$

with $[expr]$ being the Iverson bracket: $[expr] = 1$ if the enclosed expression is true, and 0 otherwise. Hence, the binary function $\max_i ([\cdot])$ detects whether there exists *any* 3D object in the scene that projects to image position $\mathbf{u}$. The marginal is approximated with samples $\mathbf{X}^{(s)}$ drawn using MCMC:

$$P(\mathbf{u}|\mathcal{E}) \approx \frac{1}{S} \sum_{s=1}^{S} \max_i \left(\left[\mathbf{u} = \mathbf{o}^{i,(s)}\right]\right) , \tag{7.11}$$

where $\mathbf{o}^{i,(s)}$ denotes the projection of object $\mathbf{O}^i$ of sample s to the image, and S is the number of samples. In practice $\max_i ([\cdot])$ checks whether any of the 3D objects of sample s projects into a small neighborhood of the image position $\mathbf{u}$.

7.3 MULTI-FRAME SCENE MODEL AND INFERENCE

So far we have described our scene model for a single image in static scenes only. For the extension to video streams we pursue a two-stage tracking approach. First, we extend the model to neighboring frames by using greedy data association. Second, the resulting *scene tracklets* are used to extend our model towards long-term data association by performing *scene tracking* with an HMM.

7.3.1 Multi-frame 3D scene tracklet model

To apply our model to multiple frames, we first use the observer's estimated speed V_{ego} and turn (yaw) rate to roughly compensate the camera's ego-motion. Next, we use a coarse dynamic model for all moving objects to locally perform association, which is refined during tracking. For initial data associations, objects that move substantially slower than the camera (e.g., people), are modeled as standing still, $V_x^i = 0$. For objects with a similar speed (e.g., cars and trucks), we distinguish those moving in the same direction as the observers from the oncoming traffic with the help of the detector's class label. The former are expected to move with a similar speed as the observer, $V_x^i = V_{ego}$, whereas the latter are expected to move with a similar speed, but in opposite direction, $V_x^i = -V_{ego}$. The camera pitch Θ_t can be assumed constant for small time intervals.

For a given frame t we associate objects and detections as described in Section 7.2.2. In adjacent frames we perform association by finding the detection with maximum overlap to each predicted object. Missing evidence is compensated by assuming a minimum detection likelihood anywhere in the image. We define the scene tracklet posterior as

$$P(\mathbf{X}_t | \mathcal{E}_{-\delta t + t : t + \delta t}) \propto \prod_{r = t - \delta t}^{t + \delta t} P(\hat{\mathbf{X}}_r | \mathcal{E}_r), \tag{7.12}$$

where $\hat{\mathbf{X}}_r$ denotes the predicted scene configuration using the initial dynamic model just explained. $P(\hat{\mathbf{X}}_r | \mathcal{E}_r)$ is defined similarly to the single frame model as

$$\begin{aligned} P(\hat{\mathbf{X}}_r | \mathcal{E}_r) &\propto \mathcal{N}(\hat{\Theta}_r; \mu_\Theta, \sigma_\Theta) \cdot \prod_i \mathcal{N}(H^i; \mu_H^{c_i}, \sigma_H^{c_i}) \cdot \Psi_D\left(\mathbf{d}_r^{a_r(i)}\right) \\ &\cdot \Psi_G\left(\hat{O}_r^i, \hat{\Theta}_r; \mathbf{d}_r^{a_r(i)}\right) \cdot \Psi_L^i\left(\hat{\mathbf{X}}_r; l_r\right). \end{aligned} \tag{7.13}$$

7.3.2 Long term data association with scene tracking

While the above model extension to scene tracklets is feasible for small time intervals, it does not scale well to longer sequences, because greedy data association in combination with a simplistic motion model will eventually fail. Moreover, the greedy formalism cannot handle objects leaving or entering the scene.

We therefore introduce an explicit data association variable $\mathcal{A}_t$, which assigns objects to detections in frame t. With this explicit mapping, long-term tracking is performed by modeling associations over time in a hidden Markov model (HMM). Inference is performed in a sliding window of length w to avoid latency as required by an online setting:

$$\begin{aligned} P(\mathbf{X}_{1:w}, \mathcal{A}_{1:w} | \mathcal{E}_{-\delta t + 1 : w + \delta t}) &= P(\mathbf{X}_1 | \mathcal{A}_1, \mathcal{E}_{-\delta t + 1 : 1 + \delta t}) \\ \prod_{k=2}^{w} P(\mathcal{A}_k | \mathcal{A}_{k-1}) P(\mathbf{X}_k | \mathcal{A}_k, \mathcal{E}_{-\delta t + k : k + \delta t}) \end{aligned} \tag{7.14}$$

The emission model is the scene tracklet model from Section 7.3.1, but with explicit data association $\mathcal{A}_k$. The transition probabilities are defined as $P(\mathcal{A}_k | \mathcal{A}_{k-1}) \propto P_e^\eta P_l^\lambda$. Thus, P_e is the probability for an object to enter the scene, while P_l denotes the probability for an object to leave the scene. To determine the number η of objects entering the scene, respectively the number λ of objects leaving the scene, we again perform frame-by-frame greedy maximum overlap matching. In Equation (7.14) the marginals $P(\mathbf{X}_k, \mathcal{A}_k | \mathcal{E}_{-\delta t + 1 : w + \delta t})$ can be computed with the sum-product algorithm (Kschischang et al., 2001). Finally, the probability of an object being part of the scene is computed by marginalization over all other variables (cf. Section 7.2.3):

$$P(\mathbf{u}_k|\mathcal{E}_{-\delta t+1:w+\delta t}) = \sum_{\mathcal{A}_k} \int \max_i \left(\left[\mathbf{u}_k = \mathbf{o}_k^i\right]\right) P(\mathbf{X}_k, \mathcal{A}_k|\mathcal{E}_{-\delta t+1:w+\delta t}) \, \mathrm{d}\mathbf{X}_k \qquad (7.15)$$

In practice we approximate the integral with MCMC samples as above, however this time only using those that correspond to the data association $\mathcal{A}_k$. Note that the summation over $\mathcal{A}_k$ only requires to consider associations that occur in the sample set.

7.4 DATASETS AND IMPLEMENTATION DETAILS

For our experiments we use two datasets: (1) *ETH-Loewenplatz*, which was introduced by Ess *et al.* (2009a) to benchmark pedestrian tracking from a moving observer; and (2) a new multi-class dataset we recorded with an onboard camera to specifically evaluate the challenges targeted by our work including realistic traffic scenarios with a large number of small objects, objects of interest from different categories, and higher driving speed.

ETH-Loewenplatz. This publicly available pedestrian benchmark[13] contains 802 frames overall at a resolution of 640×480 pixels of which every 4th frame is annotated. The sequence, which has been recorded from a driving car in urban traffic at ≈15 fps, comes with a total of 2631 annotated bounding boxes. Figure 7.6 shows some examples.

Multi-class test set. As the above dataset is restricted to pedestrians observed at low driving speeds, we recorded a new multi-class test set consisting of 674 images. The data is subdivided into 5 sequences and has been recorded at a resolution of 752×480 pixels from a driving car at ≈15 fps. Additionally ego-speed and turn rate are obtained from the car's ESP module. See Figure 7.9 for example images. The annotations consist of labeled bounding boxes for 1331 front view of cars, 156 rear view of cars, and 422 front views of trucks. Vehicles appear over a large range of scales from as small as 20 pixels to as large as 270 pixels. 46% of the objects have a height of ≤ 30 pixels, and are thus hard to detect.

Object detectors. To detect potential object instances, we use state-of-the-art object detectors. For *ETH-Loewenplatz* we obtain detection results with the detector framework presented in Chapter 4. To obtain robust detections, both gradient orientations and optic flow are used as features. SVM margins are mapped to positive values with a soft-clipping function (Dalal, 2006).

For our new test set we employ a multi-class detector based on traditional HOG-features (Dalal and Triggs, 2005) and joint boosting (Torralba *et al.*, 2007) as classifier. It can detect the four object classes *car front*, *car back*, *truck front* or *truck back*. We use a 40×40 pixel detection window, but upscale the image by a factor of 2, which turned out to perform better than a 20×20 pixel detection window. We use 4×4 pixel cells and

---

[13] http://www.vision.ee.ethz.ch/~aess/dataset/

Figure 7.3: Training samples for our multi-class object detector.

blocks of 2×2 cells. For block normalization we use the L_1-$sqrt$ norm while we have 18 histogram bins per cell and preserve the gradient direction.

Our training dataset for the multi-class vehicle detector contains 315 samples for *cars front*, 399 samples for *cars rear*, 519 samples for *truck front* and 547 samples for *trucks rear*. All images were recorded from a driving car to resemble the viewpoint as closely as possible. Figure 7.3 shows some of the training samples. Negative training data is sampled from 458 full images recorded from different environments. We employ a two-stage bootstrapping strategy in order to collect hard negative examples close to the decision boundaries.

The detection scores are mapped to positive values by means of class-wise sigmoid functions. Note that for our application it is important to explicitly separate front from back views, because the motion model is dependent on the heading direction.

Scene labeling. Every pixel is assigned to the classes *pedestrian, vehicle, street, lane marking, sky* or *void* to obtain a scene labeling. As features we use the first 16 coefficients of the Walsh-Hadamard transform extracted at five scales (4-64 pixels), along with the pixels' (x, y)-coordinates to account for their location in the image (cf. Section 6.3.1). The WHT is a discrete approximation of the cosine transform and can be computed efficiently (Hel-Or and Hel-Or, 2005; Alon et al., 2006) – on a modern GPU even in real-time.

After gray world normalization of the image, WHT features are extracted at five scales (4-64 pixels) from each channel of the CIE-*Lab* color space.

The *L*-channel is mean/variance normalized to cope with global lighting variations, whereas the *a*- and *b*-channels are normalized with the gray world assumption to mitigate color shift.

We also found that L_1-normalizing the transformation's coefficients as in Varma and Zisserman (2002) to be beneficial. We then compute mean and variance on 4×4 pixel groups and classify them with joint boosting. This classifier directly performs multi-label classification, and yields more efficient classifiers because of its capability to share features between classes. This algorithm is trained on 55 labeled ground truth images for the pedestrian dataset, respectively 56 ground truth labelings for the vehicle dataset.

Experimental setup. For both datasets and all object classes we use the same set of parameters for our MCMC sampler: $q_{Add} = 0.1$, $q_{Del} = 0.1$, $q_{Dif} = 0.8$, $q_\mathbf{O} = 0.8$, $q_\Theta = 0.2$. For the HMM's sliding window of Equation (7.14) we choose a length of $W = 7$ frames. Our sampler uses 3,000 samples for burn-in and 20,000 samples to approximate the posterior and runs without parallelization at about 1 fps on recent hardware. By running multiple Markov chains in parallel we expect a possible speed-up of one or two orders of magnitude. As we do not have 3D ground truth to assess 3D performance, we project the results back to the images and match them to ground truth annotations with the PASCAL criterion (*intersection/union* > 50%, cf. Everingham et al., 2010).

Baselines. As baselines we report both the performance of the object detectors as well as the result of an extended Kalman filter (EKF) atop the detections. The EKFs track the objects independently, but work in 3D state space with the same dynamic models as our MCMC sampler. To reduce false alarms in the absence of an explicit model for new objects entering, tracks are declared valid only after three successive associations. Analogous to our system, the camera ego-motion is compensated using odometry. Best results were obtained, when the last detection's score was used as confidence measure.

7.5 EXPERIMENTAL RESULTS

We start by reporting our system's performance for pedestrians on *ETH-Loewenplatz*. Following Ess et al. (2009a) we consider only people with a height of at least 60 pixels. The authors kindly provided us with their original results to allow for a fair comparison.[14]

In the following we analyze the performance at a constant error rate of 0.1 false positive per image (FPPI). At this error rate the detector (dotted red curve) achieves a miss rate of 48.0%, cf. Figure 7.5(a). False detections typically appear on background structures (such as trees or street signs, cf. Figure 7.6(a)) or on pedestrians' body parts. When we perform single frame inference (solid blue curve) with our model we improve by 10.4%; additionally adding tracking (dashed blue curve) performs similarly (improvement of 11.6%; see Figure 7.6, Figure 7.1(a)), but some false positives in the high precision regime are reinforced. When we omit scene labeling but use scene tracklets (black curve) of two adjacent frames our model achieves an improvement of 10.8% compared to the detector. When pixel-labeling information is added to obtain the full model (solid red curve), we observe best results with an improvement of 15.2%. Additionally performing long-term data association (dashed red curve) does not further improve the performance for this dataset: recall has already saturated due to the good performance of the detector, whereas the precision cannot be boosted because the remaining false positives happen to be consistent with the scene model (e.g., human-sized street signs).

Figure 7.5(b) compares the system's performance to EKFs and state-of-the-art results (Ess et al., 2009a). When we track detections with EKFs (yellow curve) we gain 2.5% compared to the detector, but add additional false detections in the high precision regime, as high-scoring false positives on background structures are further strengthened. Compared to their detector (HOG, Dalal and Triggs, 2005, dotted cyan curve), the system in Ess et al. (2009a) achieves an improvement of 11.1% using stereo vision (solid cyan curve), while our monocular approach gains 15.2% over the detector (cf. Chapter 4)

---

[14]The original results published in Ess et al. (2009a) were biased *against* Ess et al., because they did not allow detections slightly < 60 pixels to match true pedestrians ≥ 60 pixels, discarding many correct detections. We therefore regenerated all FPPI-curves.

110 CHAPTER 7. MONOCULAR 3D SCENE MODELING AND INFERENCE

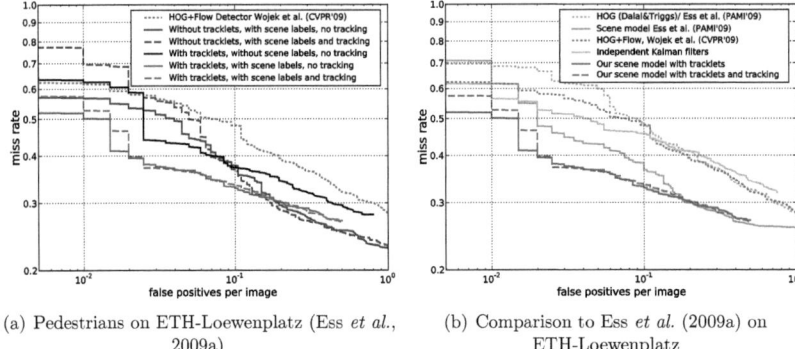

(a) Pedestrians on ETH-Loewenplatz (Ess et al., 2009a)

(b) Comparison to Ess et al. (2009a) on ETH-Loewenplatz

Figure 7.4: Results for *pedestrians* on ETH-Loewenplatz obtained with our system and comparison to the state-of-the-art. Figure best viewed in color.

used in our system. We obtain a miss rate of 32.8% using monocular video, which clearly demonstrates the power of the proposed approach using multi-frame scene tracklets in conjunction with local pixel-labeling. Some example results of our system are depicted in Figures 7.1 and 7.6. Our scene tracklet model allows to stabilize horizon estimation compared to a single-frame model, see Figure 7.1(a). Moreover, consistent detections and scene labels boost performance, especially when geometry estimation is more difficult, such as for example in the absence of a sufficient number of objects with confident detections, cf. Figures 7.6(b),(c). Figure 7.5 shows results on sample images as occupancy grid.

Next, we turn to the evaluation on our new multi-class dataset. We note, that *cars rear* are detected almost perfectly, due to the fact that there are only few instances at rather similar scales. Moreover, the test dataset does not contain rear views of trucks. Hence, we will focus on the classes *car front* and *truck front*. In the following, when we refer to cars or trucks this always concerns front views.

For cars the detector achieves a miss rate of 27.0% (see Figure 7.8(a)). Independent EKFs improve results by 1.1% to a miss rate of 25.9%. However, in the high precision regime some recall is lost. False positives mainly occur on parts of actual cars, such as on head lights of cars in the near-field, and on rear views of cars – see Figure 7.9(a). Thus, in the single-frame case of our approach the false detections are often strengthened rather than weakened by the scene geometry, cf. Figure 7.1(b), and in some cases even wrongly bias geometry estimation, thus lowering the scores for correct objects. A drop in high precision performance is the result (27.8% miss rate at 0.1 FPPI). This drop can partially be recovered to a miss rate of 21.8%, when an HMM is added for longer-term tracking.

When scene tracklets are employed, many false hypotheses are discarded because of the gross mismatch between their expected and observed dynamics. Consequently, scene tracklets boost performance significantly, resulting in an improvement of 9.9% in miss

7.5 EXPERIMENTAL RESULTS

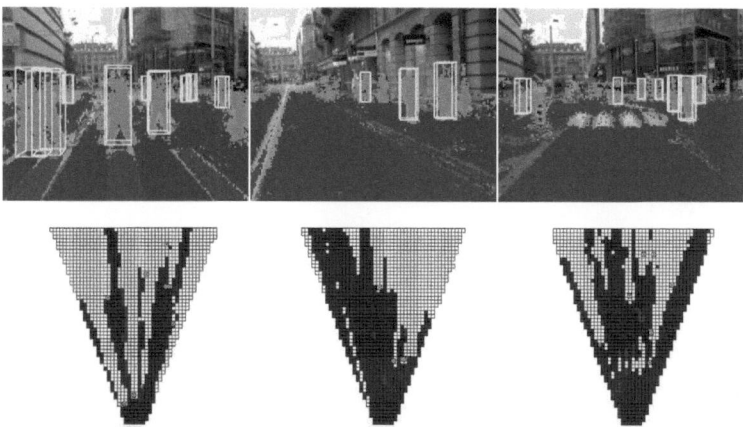

Figure 7.5: Sample results for *ETH-Loewenplatz* as occupancy grid visualization. Top row shows results projected to the image. Bottom row depicts the according bird's eye view. One grid cell corresponds to 0.5m×0.5m (maximum distance 30m).

rate. Adding long-term tracking with the HMM again only slightly improves result over scene tracklets (by 0.1%). Therefore we conclude that the critical source of improvement is *not* to track objects over extended periods of time, but to enforce a *consistent scene interpretation with short tracklets*, by tightly coupling tracklet estimation with geometry fitting and scene labeling.

Finally, we also report results for trucks, cf. Figure 7.8(b). For this class our detector has a higher miss rate of 59.4%. This is caused by a significantly higher intra-class variation among trucks and by the fact that the frontal truck detector often fires on cars due to the high visual similarity of the lower part – an example is shown in Figure 7.1(b). As a consequence, independent EKFs do not yield an improvement (miss rate 60.9%), as already observed for cars. Similarly, our model using single-frame evidence is not able to disambiguate the classes when both detectors fire, resulting in a miss rate of 67.9%. Though HMM tracking improves this to 57.6%.

As in the previous examples, our scene tracklet model is able to suppress many false detections through evidence aggregation across a small number of frames (miss rate 38.6%). Also, weak detections on small scale objects are strengthened, thus recall is improved – cf. Figures 7.9(a),(b). Compared to the detector, we improve the miss rate by 20.8%, respectively by 23.9% when also adding HMM tracking. Figure 7.8 depicts results on for some sample images from a bird's eye view.

Discussion. Overall, our experiments for two datasets and four different object classes indicate that our scene tracklet model is able to exploit scene context to robustly infer both the 3D scene geometry and the presence of objects in that scene from a monocular camera. This performance is mainly due to the use of a strong *tracking-by-detection*

Figure 7.6: Sample images showing typical results of our model along with MAP scene labels at a constant error rate of 0.1 false positives per image. *Street* pixels appear in purple, *lane markings* in light purple, *sky* in yellow, *pedestrians* in green and *vehicles* in orange. *Void* (background) pixels are not overlayed. The light green line denotes the estimated horizon.

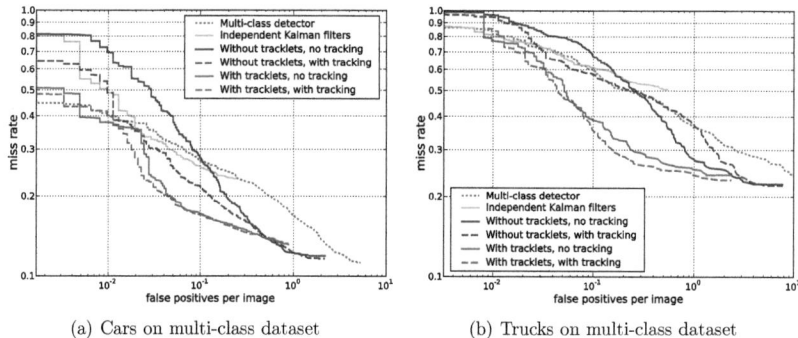

(a) Cars on multi-class dataset (b) Trucks on multi-class dataset

Figure 7.7: Results obtained with our system for *truck* and *car* on our new data set. Figure best viewed in color.

framework which employs *tracklets* on a scene level thereby leveraging evidence from a number of consecutive frames. The tight coupling with the observation model allows to exploit *3D scene context* as well as to *combine multiple cues* of a detector and from scene labeling. Long-term tracking with an HMM only results in minor additional improvement. In all cases, independent extended 3D Kalman filters cannot significantly improve the output of state-of-the-art object detectors on these datasets, and are greatly outperformed by the integrated model. On the new multi-class dataset we outperform state-of-the-art detection by 10.0% for cars, respectively 23.9% for trucks at 0.1 FPPI.

Comparing to other work that integrates detection and scene modeling, we also outperform Ess *et al.* (2009a) by 3.8% at 0.1 FPPI for the case of pedestrians, even though we do not use stereo information. At a recall of 60% our model reduces the number of false positives by almost a factor of 4.

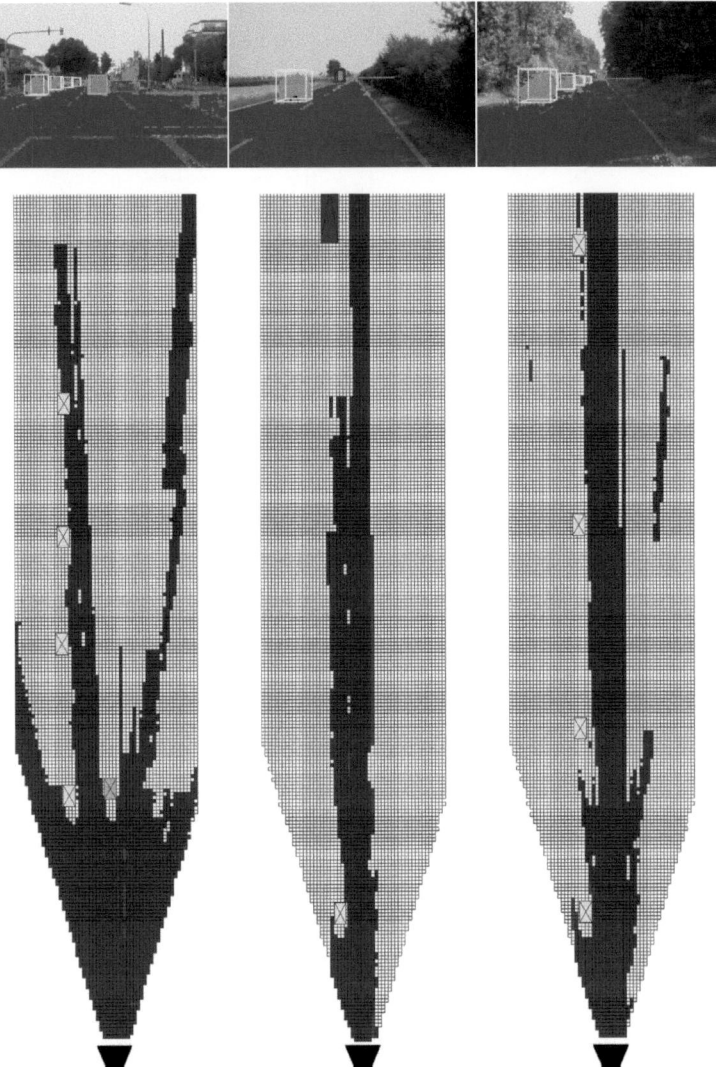

Figure 7.8: Sample results for the new multi-view dataset as occupancy grid visualization. Top row shows results projected to the image. Bottom row depicts the according bird's eye view. One grid cell corresponds to 0.5m×0.5m (maximum distance 130m).

Figure 7.9: Example images showing typical results of our model on the new multi-class dataset at a constant error rate of 0.1 false positives per image. *Street* pixels appear in purple, *lane markings* in light purple, *sky* in yellow and *vehicles* in orange. *Void* (background) pixels are not overlayed. Oncoming cars are shown with yellow bounding boxes, oncoming trucks with dark blue bounding boxes. Cars estimated as driving in the same direction appear in light blue bounding boxes. The light green line denotes the estimated horizon.

7.6 CONCLUSION

In this chapter we have presented a probabilistic 3D scene model, that enables multi-frame tracklet inference on a scene level in a tracking-by-detection framework. Our system performs monocular 3D scene geometry estimation in realistic traffic scenes, and leads to more reliable detection of objects such as pedestrians, cars, and trucks. We exploit information from object (category) detection and low-level scene labeling to obtain a *consistent 3D description of an observed scene*, even though we only use a single camera. Our experimental results show a clear improvement over top-performing state-of-the-art object detectors. Moreover, we significantly outperform basic Kalman filters and a state-of-the-art stereo camera system (Ess *et al.*, 2009a).

Our experiments underline the observation that objects are valuable constraints for the underlying 3D geometry, and vice versa (cf. Hoiem *et al.*, 2008b; Ess *et al.*, 2009a), so that a joint estimation can improve detection performance.

In future work we plan to extend our model with a more elaborate tracking framework with long-term occlusion handling. Moreover, we aim to model further components and objects of road scenes such as street markings and motorbikes. It would also be interesting to explore the fusion with complementary sensors such as RADAR or LIDAR, which should allow for further improvements.

8
CONCLUSION AND FUTURE PERSPECTIVES

Contents
    8.1 Discussion of contributions **118**
    8.2 Future perspectives **119**

THIS thesis investigated the automatic understanding of visual scenes in realistic environments from a single monocular camera's video. In particular, we focused on *robotics* and *driver assistance* application scenarios. We improved state-of-the-art performance with respect to multiple relevant aspects. These include object detection, semantic scene labeling and 3D scene understanding. For each task we developed models for static images as well as for videos. All approaches were evaluated on realistic data sets to show our models' effectiveness. Where no established data set was available, we recorded own data and made it publicly available.

We noted that the detection of objects is an important subtask for the automated analysis of visual scenes as they allow to heavily constrain the scene's context. For instance, one common assumption is that objects stand on a common ground plane. Therefore, a more robust detection of objects allow to improve the understanding of full scenes.

As a running example the detection of pedestrians and vehicles was used throughout this thesis. We conducted a thorough analysis of different feature and classifier combinations for the sliding window detection framework and found that the combination of complementary features allows to substantially improve results. We also showed that exploiting the parallel capabilities of recent commodity graphics hardware allows to fulfill real-time requirements even for highly dynamic applications such as driver assistance on highways.

With a powerful object detector in hand we proposed two scene models, which exploit *context* on two different levels. The first one addresses the task of scene understanding on the 2D image by semantic pixel-wise labeling. Here the *semantic* context is constituted by the local neighborhood of the image patch to be classified. We showed that a joint model which incorporates low-level texture features and object hypotheses allows to improve segmentation performance. Further improvements were possible when single frame posterior distributions were propagated as *temporal* context to the next time step's image.

The second scene model we presented, jointly infers the 3D scene consisting of object positions and the camera geometry by using monocular video only. This model offers object-object and object-camera interactions and thus the notion of *geometric 3D* context extends to the entire scene. The previously described semantic scene labels and a set of object detections are required as input. We showed that a tight coupling of tracking-by-detection (*temporal* context) and scene estimation (*geometric 3D* context) by the notion of *scene tracklets* allows to substantially improve the object detector's performance even though only a single camera has been used.

In particular, the joint 3D scene model's results are encouraging, but further progress is necessary in order to deploy the proposed techniques in real environments. Our results suggest that improved long-term tracking in conjunction with extended 3D reasoning for occlusion handling are very promising directions towards real systems. Further restrictions such as limitations in runtime performance can be overcome by application-specific implementations on parallel hardware.

8.1 DISCUSSION OF CONTRIBUTIONS

The overall goal of this thesis was to robustly infer entire scenes for real world applications (1) in order to explicitly determine free space and (2) to determine the positions of all relevant objects. This thesis contributes several steps towards these goals, which are important to facilitate (semi-)autonomous navigation in complex environments.

Firstly, Chapter 3 conducted an extensive study of people detection with a sliding window framework. It evaluated different static features (i.e., features computed on a single image) and their combination. Contrary to most previous works, different classifiers and combinations of features were evaluated. While most works use the false positive per window (FPPW) metric for evaluation we suggested improved evaluation metrics based on full image detection performance. We showed that those allow a better assessment of a detection system's performance. We discussed several shortcomings of the FPPW metric and experimentally showed that it might fail to predict the true performance. Accordingly, several results published in the literature overestimated algorithm performance, which has been acknowledged by some authors in the meanwhile[15,16]. Furthermore, we have shown that a new object descriptor based on the dense sampling of shape context (Belongie et al., 2002) can achieve similar performance to other state-of-the-art descriptors (e.g., Dalal and Triggs, 2005).

Next, Chapter 4 investigated onboard pedestrian detection from a moving platform. It also included motion features and MPLBoost (Babenko et al., 2008) as additional classifier. The common intuition is that a moving camera might impede a performance improvement by motion features. However, we experimentally showed improved results when differences in the optic flow field are encoded as features. In particular pedestrians moving perpendicularly to the camera can be detected more robustly. Due to their high likelihood of crossing the camera's trajectory these are of primary interest for driver assistance applications. While our features are similar to Dalal et al. (2006), we addressed several unresolved issues mentioned in Dalal (2006). In particular, we showed how to adapt the non-maximum suppression step in order to improve the motion feature-based detection performance compared to static feature only detection. We also

---

[15]http://www.cs.sfu.ca/~mori/research/papers/sabzmeydani_shapelet_cvpr07.html
[16]http://www.cs.berkeley.edu/~smaji/projects/ped-detector/

showed, that MPLBoost provides more robust classification results than traditional AdaBoost and underlined its applicability for pedestrian detection.

Real-time processing is a major issue for the deployment of real-world computer vision applications. In highly dynamic scenarios, e.g., driver assistance on highways, this requires to process up to 20 images per second. In order to achieve this runtime performance the case study in Chapter 5 showed that sliding window detection frameworks can be sped up by almost two orders of magnitudes (compared to CPU implementations) when algorithmic parallelism is exploited. We showed that one of the top-performing people detectors (Dalal and Triggs, 2005) can be run with graphics hardware (GPU) support at a frame rate of more than 20 Hz on VGA (640×480 pixels) images without a loss in detection performance.

The task of explicitly identifying free space is addressed in Chapter 6 by pixel-wise scene labeling in a CRF framework. One major shortcoming of the standard CRF formulation on a 2D lattice is that classes with a low data fraction are easily misclassified due to a low impact on the optimized objective function. Another shortcoming is that most works use only 4-connected neighborhoods as these are computationally tractable for very dense local neighborhood interactions. Thus, we proposed to exploit object hypotheses retrieved from an object detector to instantiate additional object nodes in the CRF. These nodes allow a tighter variable coupling and enable longer range interactions. Moreover, they allow to incorporate the detector's confidence, which is more robust than the local patch classification confidence computed from texture features. We further extended this model by means of a temporal formulation to a dynamic CRF. To account for different dynamics of objects and the remaining scene we introduced different dynamic models. Our overall results indicated, that both – static and dynamic – CRF models enable a better image segmentation.

Finally, Chapter 7 proposed a 3D scene model which is based on the tracking-by-detection paradigm to further improve object detection reliability. Our 3D model is inferred from a single camera's view, while most previous work used stereo cameras for this task (e.g., Ess *et al.*, 2009a; Gavrila and Munder, 2007). It draws its strength from the tight coupling of the following components. First, 3D scene context ensures consistency among all detections with respect to size and position within the scene. Second, semantic scene labeling information allows to discard inconsistent false detections, while the 3D model allows to model object-object occlusions. And third, scene tracklets allow to strengthen temporally consistent detections. To perform inference we resorted to a MCMC scheme with reversible jumps. We showed that in particular the semantic scene labeling and the use of scene tracklets allow to boost the detector's performance. In terms of detection performance we outperformed the plain detector, standard Kalman filters as well as another state-of-the-art system (Ess *et al.*, 2009a) which is based on stereo cameras. Results were shown on several realistic vehicle and pedestrian datasets.

8.2 FUTURE PERSPECTIVES

Throughout this thesis we were able to improve the state-of-the-art automated visual scene understanding with respect to recognition and runtime performance. However, robustness and reliability still need to be advanced in order to deploy real systems and thus further research is required. In particular the system proposed in Chapter 7 is amenable to various extensions and is therefore a good starting point for further development. The following section will discuss some possible directions for future work.

Detection on low resolution images. Our recent performance evaluation for pedestrian detection (Dollár et al., 2009b) on an extensive onboard dataset has shown that all algorithms tested achieve insufficient detection performance on small scales (i.e., when the resolution is ≤ 30 pixels). Most research so far has concentrated to model pedestrians with a height of around 100 pixels and managed to detect smaller instances by upscaling the input image. The major problem on small scales is the limited image evidence and it is unclear how small instances can be detected more reliably. While scene models, as proposed in this thesis, alleviate false detections errors, they are usually unable to increase recall. One direction for future research is to model pedestrians with different models and features for the detection on different scales. Another one is the investigation of different features which might be better suited for the detection on small scales.

Multi-cue object detection. While this thesis has shown that the combination of different static features or the combination with flow features can be beneficial, further sources of information can be exploited to increase detection robustness. Stereo vision might for instance provide valuable and complementary information. Additionally, different ways of encoding optic flow information in an ego-motion invariant way might be a promising research direction.

Instance-specific models for (re-)detecting people. In this thesis we addressed the task of detecting objects with object-class models, which were general in a sense that they aimed to detect any object of the trained class. Other works (Avidan, 2007; Grabner and Bischof, 2006; Babenko et al., 2009) perform robust tracking by learning an instance-specific object model, dedicated to detect a single object instance. These models are however usually hand-initialized and are often subject to drift. Ideally the begin of a track would start from the detections of a powerful general object-class detector and then be refined to some extent to a specific object instance. Pedestrian models might additionally adapt to the human motion cycle. The danger however is, that also false detections might be reinforced by such a model refinement. First attempts towards more adaptive models have been proposed by Andriluka et al. (2008) and Grabner et al. (2008). Similar ideas of adaption might be reused in surveillance applications to track and re-identify people across cameras in larger networks.

Multi-viewpoint object detection. In parts of this thesis we have used detectors which were trained to detect objects from a specific viewpoint (e.g., the rears of cars). Many applications will however require the robust detection of objects from many viewpoints. For pedestrians we have proposed to use the MPLBoost classification framework with the intuition to automatically cluster viewpoints and to learn view-specific detectors within the training process in an unsupervised way. It

8.2 FUTURE PERSPECTIVES

is unclear however, how performance compares to hand-crafted viewpoint-specific detectors which are trained in a fully supervised way from viewpoint annotations or to detector hierarchies (e.g., Gavrila, 2007). Moreover, the discretization of the viewing sphere with viewpoint-specific detectors learned for each individual viewpoint seems suboptimal and computationally more efficient models are desirable. Hence, further studies are required to solve the problem of multi-viewpoint object detection. For human detection, a successful viewpoint estimate will also allow to initialize dynamic models more robustly and to retrieve the human pose and heading direction more accurately (cf., Andriluka et al., 2010).

Multi-class object detection. The efficient detection of a larger number of object-classes is a further open problem. While we successfully detected vehicle classes as well as pedestrians in this thesis, the number of relevant object classes for future applications is much higher. Even though the feature representation might be reused, future classifiers in object detectors must be able to handle far more object classes. Torralba et al. (2007) proposed to share features between classes in a boosting framework. However, when this classifier is used in conjunction with a sliding window approach (cf. Chapter 7) all classes need to be modeled with a fixed aspect ratio and at the same scale, which might often be suboptimal. Classifier cascades (Zehnder et al., 2008) which were successfully used to speed up indivial object class detection might be one way to improve runtime performance.

Application-specific hardware implementations. In this thesis we have shown that state-of-the-art object detectors can in principle be run in real-time when graphic co-processors are used. For realistic onboard applications GPUs are often difficult to realize due to the relatively high demands in terms of power consumption. Nonetheless, similar parallel programming techniques can be used for application-specific hardware development on devices such as field programmable gate arrays (FPGA). Further speed-ups are possible when prior knowledge is used for the sliding window scanning process (e.g., Gerónimo et al., 2005). A rough scene model might for example restrict the scanned image regions depending on the object scale (i.e., the sky and the close-range are not scanned for small object scales). Moreover, features which are computationally less demanding (e.g., Dollár et al., 2009a), but nonetheless yield good performance might replace the current histograms of oriented gradients.

Dynamic models for scene segmentation. Our scene model for 2D scene segmentation (Chapter 6) used an idealistic flat world assumption, which turned out to yield satisfying results. However, this assumption can be replaced with more elaborate dynamic models to propagate the background scene classes. Propagation based on stereo depth estimation or based on an optic flow field should improve results. Additionally, objects were modeled without mutual interactions. An underlying scene model as presented in Chapter 7 might address this issue and could be integrated with the segmentation framework.

Improved tracking and occlusion handling. The scene model presented in Chapter 7 employed a hidden Markov model for tracking and long-term data association. While this tracking scheme allowed to improve results in some cases it does not allow to handle occlusions. More advanced techniques, which for instance could exploit the available 3D information, are required. Occlusion models for object-object occlusion can directly be extracted from 3D positions. Detectors for parts of humans (e.g., upper body) might be a further extension to cope with occlusion from other objects such as, e.g., street furniture. Without a scene model these detectors will presumably have a substantially higher false positive rate. But including them in a scene model as additional evidence might help to further improve the detection rate. Further extensions to the current model are more realistic dynamic models (e.g., Kalman filters; Pellegrini *et al.*, 2009) and an entry and exit model to improve object handling close to the image boundary.

Scene model extensions. Further extensions to the proposed scene model are possible. For driver assistance and robotics applications these include modeling of further components such as buildings or the drivable surface. A more complete set of object classes, e.g., including bicyclists or tractors will make the model more realistic. Even though the models in this thesis were developed for monocular cameras the extension to stereo cameras is possible and stereo disparity will be a further useful cue. In addition, stereo information might help to model unknown (i.e., obstacles of classes for which no detector is available) object classes. Moreover, it might be possible to relax the flat ground plane assumption and extract a more accurate surface from stereo information (cf. Wedel *et al.*, 2009).

Evaluation of 3D accuracy. While we proposed a 3D scene model in this thesis its evaluation in terms of 3D localization accuracy turned out to be difficult. The major issue is how to reliable determine the ground truth without reducing the complexity of the application scenario. Up-to-date this problem is unresolved and needs further investigation. Clearly an evaluation with respect to 3D accuracy would be very valuable for several applications which rely on a scene model to autonomously control a vehicle or robot.

Sensor fusion. Recognition performance for cameras working in the visual spectrum of light constantly improved throughout the last years. However, only in few cases the application requirements in terms of robustness and reliability are so far met by systems relying only on visual light sensors. Therefore, fusion with complementary sensors is a promising direction to improve overall system performance. The additional sensors which are partially already deployed in current applications can be grouped as follows. *Visual sensors* such as infrared or time-of-flight cameras can be employed for night time vision or for a more reliable depth estimate. *Ray sensors* such as RADAR, laser or ultra sonic sensors are robust to difficult lighting conditions and therefore often used in combination with visual sensors. *Maps* allow to extract additional prior information and are so far rarely exploited. Tracking for instance might set up or end car tracks on junctions with a higher probability. Finally, *communication devices* such as car-to-car communication or infrastructure-to-car communication can provide additional sensor information which is recorded from a different viewpoint and therefore could address object occlusion. In a joint publication (Hohm *et al.*, 2008) within the research project PRORETA, we fused visual object detections and RADAR targets in a Kalman filter framework and found improved performance through sensor complementary. Visual detections improved the lateral resolution, while Doppler RADAR improved the depth and velocity estimate. Future work will not only fuse sensors for individual object tracking, but embed all sensor information in a single scene model.

LIST OF FIGURES

Fig. 1.1	An identical pattern perceived as car or pedestrian depending on the image context.	2
(a)	Object pattern perceived as car	2
(b)	Object pattern perceived as pedestrian	2
Fig. 1.2	Pedestrians with different articulations: standing, walking and running	5
Fig. 1.3	Pedestrians with varying appearance across different viewpoints, individual clothing style and physique	5
Fig. 1.4	Pedestrians carrying accessories and occlusions complicate the detection task.	6
Fig. 1.5	Typical street scenes containing objects with a large scale range.	6
Fig. 1.6	Urban environments are particularly challenging due to cluttered background and distracting background objects.	7
Fig. 1.7	Real-world scenarios need to cope with changing weather and lighting conditions.	7
Fig. 1.8	Number of image pixel rows a 10m stretch on the ground plane is projected to dependent on the distance from the camera	8
Fig. 1.9	Locally extracted evidence needs to be put in context to yield global scene understanding.	9
Fig. 3.1	Performance of available detector binaries and our implementations.	44
Fig. 3.2	Recall-Precision detector performances with single features	48
(a)	Feature performance with AdaBoost	48
(b)	Feature performance with linear SVM	48
(c)	Feature performance with RBF SVM	48
Fig. 3.3	Recall-Precision detector performances with multiple features	49
(a)	Combination of Haar wavelets (Papageorgiou and Poggio, 2000) and HOG, different classifiers	49
(b)	Combination of Haar wavelets (Papageorgiou and Poggio, 2000) and dense Shape Context, different classifiers	49
(c)	Combination Haar wavelets (Papageorgiou and Poggio, 2000), HOG and dense Shape Context, different classifiers	49
Fig. 3.4	Bootstrapped single feature detectors of Figure 3.4(b) and their combination, linear SVM	50
Fig. 3.5	Sample detections at a precision of 80%	51
Fig. 3.6	Missed recall (upper row) and false positive detections (lower row) at equal error rate	52
Fig. 4.1	Detections obtained with our detector in an urban environment	57
Fig. 4.2	Impact of flow algorithm and detection window size	59
(a)	Performance for different flow algorithms	59
(b)	Performance drops when using a smaller detection window.	59

Fig. 4.3		Bootstrapping from false detections on parts and optic flow color coding	61
	(a)	False positive detections with high scores before the bootstrapping stage	61
	(b)	Visualization color coding for flow direction and magnitude	61
Fig. 4.4		Positive sample crops and flow fields of *TUD-MotionPairs*	63
Fig. 4.5		Optic flow fields and sample detections on the *TUD-Brussels* onboard dataset at equal error rate	64
Fig. 4.6		Sample detections at 0.5 FPPI on ETH-Person dataset	65
Fig. 4.7		Sample detections for the different models learned by MPLBoost (K=4) using HOG, Haar, IMHwd	66
Fig. 4.8		Results obtained with different combinations of features and classifiers on ETH-01 and ETH-02 (Ess *et al.*, 2007)	67
	(a)	Static image features (ETH-01)	67
	(b)	Static image features (ETH-02)	67
	(c)	Including motion features (ETH-01)	67
	(d)	Including motion features (ETH-02)	67
	(e)	Comparison to Ess *et al.* (2007) (ETH-01)	67
	(f)	Comparison to Ess *et al.* (2007) (ETH-02)	67
Fig. 4.9		Results obtained with different combinations of features and classifiers on ETH-03 (Ess *et al.*, 2007) and *TUD-Brussels*	68
	(a)	Static image features (ETH-03)	68
	(b)	Static image features (*TUD-Brussels*)	68
	(c)	Including motion features (ETH-03)	68
	(d)	Including motion features (*TUD-Brussels*)	68
	(e)	Comparison to Ess *et al.* (2007) (ETH-03)	68
	(f)	Comparison of non-maximum suppression scoring methods	68
Fig. 4.10		Comparion of recall for different pedestrian sizes at a precision of 90%	69
	(a)	Recall vs. Size at 90% precision with static image features only	69
	(b)	Recall vs. Size at 90% precision including motion features	69
Fig. 5.1		Sliding window object localization using HOG descriptors	74
	(a)	HOG descriptor	74
	(b)	Computation steps	74
Fig. 5.2		Effective GPU times and calling overheads	78
Fig. 5.3		Sample detections on the INRIA Person dataset	80
Fig. 5.4		Sample detections on the TUD Dynamic Scenes (TUDDS) dataset	80
Fig. 5.5		Detection performance on the INRIA Person test set	81
Fig. 5.6		Detection performance on the TUDDS test set	81
Fig. 5.7		Increasing downscale factor on the INRIA person test set	84
Fig. 6.1		Graphical models for *object CRF* and *dynamic CRF*	89
	(a)	Graphical model for the *object CRF*	89
	(b)	Graphical model for our full *dynamic CRF*	89
Fig. 6.2		Gray world assumption for input image normalization	92
Fig. 6.3		First Walsh-Hadamard filterbank kernels and its efficient computation	92

	(a)	First 16 filter kernels of the Walsh-Hadamard transform	92
	(b)	Tree structure for efficient Walsh-Hadamard transform computation(Hel-Or and Hel-Or, 2005)	92
Fig. 6.4		*Sowerby* dataset example results	94
Fig. 6.5		*Dynamic scenes* dataset example scene labeling results and corresponding detections	97
Fig. 7.1		3D scene inference sample results	100
Fig. 7.2		Visualization of the 3D scene state **X** in the world coordinate system	102
Fig. 7.3		Training samples for our multi-class object detector.	108
Fig. 7.4		Results for *pedestrians* on ETH-Loewenplatz obtained with our system and comparison to the state-of-the-art	110
	(a)	Pedestrians on ETH-Loewenplatz (Ess *et al.*, 2009a)	110
	(b)	Comparison to Ess *et al.* (2009a) on ETH-Loewenplatz	110
Fig. 7.5		Sample results for *ETH-Loewenplatz* as occupancy grid visualization	111
Fig. 7.6		Sample images showing typical results of our model along with MAP scene labels at a constant error rate of 0.1 false positives per image	112
Fig. 7.7		Results obtained with our system for *truck* and *car* on our new data set	113
	(a)	Cars on multi-class dataset	113
	(b)	Trucks on multi-class dataset	113
Fig. 7.8		Sample results for the new multi-view dataset as occupancy grid visualization	114
Fig. 7.9		Example images showing typical results of our model on the new multi-class dataset at a constant error rate of 0.1 false positives per image	115

LIST OF TABLES

Tab. 3.1	Original combination of features and classifiers	43
Tab. 3.2	Number of images and instances for the INRIA Person dataset . . .	46
Tab. 5.1	Overview on maximum occupancy per kernel	76
Tab. 5.2	Overview on detector parameters for pedestrian and car detection .	82
(a)	Detector settings for pedestrian detection	82
(b)	Detector settings for car detection	82
Tab. 5.3	Comparison of CPU and GPU runtimes for people detection for different steps of the algorithm	83
Tab. 5.4	Comparison of CPU and GPU runtimes for car detection for different steps of the algorithm	83
Tab. 6.1	Comparison to previously reported results on the Sowerby dataset .	93
Tab. 6.2	Evaluation of texture location features based on overall pixel-wise accuracy	95
Tab. 6.3	Pixel-wise recall and precision for the pixels labeled as *car* and overall accuracy on all classes	95
Tab. 6.4	Confusion matrix for the *dynamic scenes* dataset	96

BIBLIOGRAPHY

S. Agarwal, A. Awan, and D. Roth (2004). Learning to Detect Objects in Images via a Sparse, Part-Based Representation, *IEEE Transactions on Pattern Analysis and Machine Intelligence*, vol. 26(11), pp. 1475–1490. 18, 26

S. Agarwal and D. Roth (2002). Learning a Sparse Representation for Object Detection, in *Proceedings of the European Conference on Computer Vision (ECCV) 2002*. 19

Y. Alon, A. Ferencz, and A. Shashua (2006). Off-road Path Following using Region Classification and Geometric Projection Constraints, in *Proceedings of the IEEE Conference on Computer Vision and Pattern Recognition (CVPR) 2006*. 31, 32, 92, 108

M. Andriluka, S. Roth, and B. Schiele (2008). People-Tracking-by-Detection and People-Detection-by-Tracking, in *Proceedings of the IEEE Conference on Computer Vision and Pattern Recognition (CVPR) 2008*. 36, 120

M. Andriluka, S. Roth, and B. Schiele (2009). Pictorial Structures Revisited: People Detection and Articulated Pose Estimation, in *Proceedings of the IEEE Conference on Computer Vision and Pattern Recognition (CVPR) 2009*. 17

M. Andriluka, S. Roth, and B. Schiele (2010). Monocular 3D Pose Estimation and Tracking by Detection, in *Proceedings of the IEEE Conference on Computer Vision and Pattern Recognition (CVPR) 2010*. 121

S. Avidan (2007). Ensemble Tracking, *IEEE Transactions on Pattern Analysis and Machine Intelligence*, vol. 29(2), pp. 261–271. 34, 120

B. Babenko, P. Dollár, Z. Tu, and S. Belongie (2008). Simultaneous Learning and Alignment: Multi-Instance and Multi-Pose Learning, in *ECCV Faces in Real-Life Images 2008*. 10, 56, 60, 118

B. Babenko, M.-H. Yang, and S. J. Belongie (2009). Visual tracking with online Multiple Instance Learning, in *Proceedings of the IEEE Conference on Computer Vision and Pattern Recognition (CVPR) 2009*. 34, 120

H. Badino, U. Franke, and R. Mester (2007). Free Space Computation Using Stochastic Occupancy Grids and Dynamic Programming, in *ICCV Workshop on Dynamical Vision (WDV) 2007*. 37

M. Bajracharya, B. Moghaddam, A. Howard, S. Brennan, and L. H. Matthies (2009). A Fast Stereo-based System for Detecting and Tracking Pedestrians from a Moving Vehicle, *The International Journal of Robotics Research*, vol. 28. 39, 40

Y. Bar-Shalom and T. E. Fortmann (1988). *Tracking and Data Association*, Academic Press. 33

S. Belongie, J. Malik, and J. Puzicha (2002). Shape Matching and Object Recognition Using Shape Contexts, *IEEE Transactions on Pattern Analysis and Machine Intelligence*, vol. 24(4), pp. 509–522. 10, 11, 17, 18, 41, 42, 45, 118

J. Berclaz, F. Fleuret, and P. Fua (2009). Multiple Object Tracking using Flow Linear Programming, in *IEEE International Workshop on Performance Evaluation of Tracking and Surveillance (Winter-PETS) 2009*. 35

M. Bertozzi, A. Broggi, C. Caraffi, M. D. Rose, M. Felisa, and G. Vezzoni (2007). Pedestrian detection by means of far-infrared stereo vision, *Computer Vision and Image Understanding*, vol. 106(2-3), pp. 194–204. 24

M. Betke, E. Haritaoglu, and L. S. Davis (2000). Real-time Multiple Vehicle Tracking from a Moving Vehicle, *Machine Vision and Applications*, vol. 12(2), pp. 69–83. 38

T. Binford (1982). Survey of Model-Based Image Analysis Systems, *The International Journal of Robotics Research*, vol. 1(1), pp. 18–64. 15

C. M. Bishop (2006). *Pattern Recognition and Machine Learning*, Springer. 15

A. Bissacco, M.-H. Yang, and S. Soatto (2006). Detecting Humans via Their Pose, in *Advances in Neural Information Processing Systems (NIPS) 2006*. 21

G. Borgefors (1988). Hierarchical Chamfer Matching: a Parametric Edge Matching Algorithm, *IEEE Transactions on Pattern Analysis and Machine Intelligence*, vol. 10, pp. 849–865. 18

M. D. Breitenstein, F. Reichlin, B. Leibe, E. Koller-Meier, and L. Van Gool (2009). Robust Tracking-by-Detection using a Detector Confidence Particle Filter, in *Proceedings of the IEEE International Conference on Computer Vision (ICCV) 2009*. 34

M. D. Breitenstein, E. Sommerlade, B. Leibe, L. Van Gool, and I. Reid (2008). Probabilistic Parameter Selection for Learning Scene Structure from Video, in *Proceedings of the British Machine Vision Conference (BMVC) 2008*. 37

A. Broggi, M. Bertozzi, A. Fascioli, and M. Sechi (2000). Shape-based Pedestrian Detection, in *Proceedings of the IEEE International Conference on Intelligent Vehicles (IV) 2000*. 22

G. Brostow, J. Shotton, J. Fauqueur, and R. Cipolla (2008). Segmentation and Recognition using SfM Point Clouds, in *Proceedings of the European Conference on Computer Vision (ECCV) 2008*. 31, 32

Y. Cai, N. de Freitas, and J. J. Little (2006). Robust Visual Tracking for Multiple Targets, in *Proceedings of the European Conference on Computer Vision (ECCV) 2006*. 33

J. Canny (1986). A Computational Approach to Edge Detection, *IEEE Transactions on Pattern Analysis and Machine Intelligence*, vol. 8(6), pp. 679–698. 45

P. Carbonetto, N. de Freitas, and K. Barnard (2004). A statistical model for general contextual object recognition, in *Proceedings of the European Conference on Computer Vision (ECCV) 2004*. 29

D. Comaniciu (2003). An Algorithm for Data-Driven Bandwidth Selection, *IEEE Transactions on Pattern Analysis and Machine Intelligence*, vol. 25(2), pp. 281–288. 46, 61, 72, 77

D. Comaniciu, V. Ramesh, and P. Meer (2000). Real-Time Tracking of Non-Rigid Objects Using Mean Shift, in *Proceedings of the IEEE Conference on Computer Vision and Pattern Recognition (CVPR) 2000*. 33, 34

N. Cornelis, B. Leibe, K. Cornelis, and L. Van Gool (2008). 3D Urban Scene Modeling Integrating Recognition and Reconstruction, *International Journal of Computer Vision*, vol. 78(2-3), pp. 121–141. 39

H. Dahlkamp, A. Kaehler, D. Stavens, S. Thrun, and G. R. Bradski (2006). Self-supervised Monocular Road Detection in Desert Terrain, in *Robotics: Science and Systems 2006*. 37

N. Dalal (2006). *Finding people in images and videos*, Ph.D. thesis, Institut National Polytechnique de Grenoble. 23, 56, 61, 65, 69, 74, 107, 118

N. Dalal and B. Triggs (2005). Histograms of Oriented Gradients for Human Detection, in *Proceedings of the IEEE Conference on Computer Vision and Pattern Recognition (CVPR) 2005*. 10, 11, 21, 22, 23, 27, 32, 34, 39, 41, 42, 43, 44, 46, 49, 51, 56, 58, 62, 71, 72, 79, 81, 88, 93, 107, 109, 118, 119

N. Dalal, B. Triggs, and C. Schmid (2006). Human Detection Using Oriented Histograms of Flow and Appearance, in *Proceedings of the European Conference on Computer Vision (ECCV) 2006*. 10, 23, 27, 55, 56, 58, 69, 118

A. Dempster, N. Laird, and D. Rubin (1977). Maximum likelihood from incomplete data via the EM algorithm, *Journal of the Royal Statistical Society, Series B*, vol. 39(1), pp. 1–38. 17

E. Dickmanns (2007). *Dynamic Vision for Perception and Control of Motion*, Springer. 38

S. K. Divvala, D. Hoiem, J. H. Hays, A. A. Efros, and M. Hebert (2009). An Empirical Study of Context in Object Detection, in *Proceedings of the IEEE Conference on Computer Vision and Pattern Recognition (CVPR) 2009*. 16

P. Dollár, B. Babenko, S. Belongie, P. Perona, and Z. Tu (2008). Multiple Component Learning for Object Detection, in *Proceedings of the European Conference on Computer Vision (ECCV) 2008*. 25, 56

P. Dollár, Z. Tu, P. Perona, and S. Belongie (2009a). Integral Channel Features, in *Proceedings of the British Machine Vision Conference (BMVC) 2009*. 24, 121

P. Dollár, Z. Tu, H. Tao, and S. Belongie (2007). Feature Mining For Image Classification, in *Proceedings of the IEEE Conference on Computer Vision and Pattern Recognition (CVPR) 2007*. 22, 24

P. Dollár, C. Wojek, B. Schiele, and P. Perona (2009b). Pedestrian Detection: A Benchmark, in *Proceedings of the IEEE Conference on Computer Vision and Pattern Recognition (CVPR) 2009*. 12, 26, 27, 41, 42, 47, 63, 120

B. A. Draper, R. T. Collins, J. Brolio, A. R. Hanson, and E. M. Riseman (1989). The schema system, *International Journal of Computer Vision*, vol. 2(3), pp. 209–250. 29

A. Elgammal, D. Harwood, and L. Davis (2000). Non-Parametric Model for Background Subtraction, in *Proceedings of the European Conference on Computer Vision (ECCV) 2000*. 9, 55

M. Enzweiler and D. M. Gavrila (2009). Monocular Pedestrian Detection: Survey and Experiments, *IEEE Transactions on Pattern Analysis and Machine Intelligence*. 26, 42

M. Enzweiler, P. Kanter, and D. Gavrila (2008). Monocular Pedestrian Recognition Using Motion Parallax, in *Proceedings of the IEEE International Conference on Intelligent Vehicles (IV) 2008*. 23

A. Ess, B. Leibe, K. Schindler, and L. Van Gool (2008). A Mobile Vision System for Robust Multi-Person Tracking, in *Proceedings of the IEEE Conference on Computer Vision and Pattern Recognition (CVPR) 2008*. 9, 39, 62

A. Ess, B. Leibe, K. Schindler, and L. Van Gool (2009a). Robust Multi-Person Tracking From a Mobile Platform, *IEEE Transactions on Pattern Analysis and Machine Intelligence*, vol. 31(10), pp. 1831–1846. 39, 40, 99, 100, 107, 109, 110, 113, 116, 119, 127

A. Ess, B. Leibe, and L. Van Gool (2007). Depth and Appearance for Mobile Scene Analysis, in *Proceedings of the IEEE International Conference on Computer Vision (ICCV) 2007*. 39, 55, 62, 63, 65, 66, 67, 68, 69, 126

A. Ess, T. Müller, H. Grabner, and L. Van Gool (2009b). Segmentation-Based Urban Traffic Scene Understanding, in *Proceedings of the British Machine Vision Conference (BMVC) 2009*. 31

M. Everingham, L. Van Gool, C. K. I. Williams, J. Winn, and A. Zisserman (2010). The Pascal Visual Object Classes (VOC) Challenge, *International Journal of Computer Vision*, vol. 88(2), pp. 303–338. 19, 46, 79, 85, 109

P. Felzenszwalb and D. Huttenlocher (2000). Efficient Matching of Pictorial Structures, in *Proceedings of the IEEE Conference on Computer Vision and Pattern Recognition (CVPR) 2000*. 17, 42

P. Felzenszwalb, D. McAllester, and D. Ramanan (2008). A Discriminatively Trained, Multiscale, Deformable Part Model, in *Proceedings of the IEEE Conference on Computer Vision and Pattern Recognition (CVPR) 2008*. 25, 56

P. F. Felzenszwalb, R. B. Girshick, D. McAllester, and D. Ramanan (2009). Object Detection with Discriminatively Trained Part Based Models, *IEEE Transactions on Pattern Analysis and Machine Intelligence*, vol. 99(PrePrints). 25, 39

P. F. Felzenszwalb and D. P. Huttenlocher. (2004). Efficient Graph-Based Image Segmentation, *International Journal of Computer Vision*, vol. 59(2), pp. 167–181. 28

R. Fergus, P. Perona, and A. Zisserman (2007). Weakly Supervised Scale-Invariant Learning of Models for Visual Recognition, *International Journal of Computer Vision*, vol. 71(3), pp. 273–303. 17

V. Ferrari, L. Fevrier, F. Jurie, and C. Schmid (2008). Groups of Adjacent Contour Segments for Object Detection, *IEEE Transactions on Pattern Analysis and Machine Intelligence*, vol. 30(1), pp. 36–51. 18

M. Fink and P. Perona (2003). Mutual Boosting for Contextual Inference, in *Advances in Neural Information Processing Systems (NIPS) 2003*. 28

M. A. Fischler and R. A. Elschlager (1973). The Representation and Matching of Pictorial Structures, *IEEE Transactions on Computer*, vol. 22(1), pp. 67–92. 17

R. A. Fisher (1936). The use of multiple measurements in taxonomic problems, *Annals of Eugenics*, vol. 7, pp. 179–188. 21

W. Förstner and E. Gülch (1987). A fast operator for detection and precise location of distinct points, corners and centres of circular features, in *ISPRS Intercommission Conference on Fast Processing of Photogrammetric Data 1987*. 17, 18

D. Forsyth and M. Fleck (1997). Body plans, in *Proceedings of the IEEE Conference on Computer Vision and Pattern Recognition (CVPR) 1997*. 17, 42

U. Franke and A. Joos (2000). Real-Time Stereo Vision for Urban Traffic Scene Understanding, in *Proceedings of the IEEE International Conference on Intelligent Vehicles (IV) 2000*. 39

J. Friedman, T. Hastie, and R. Tibshirani (2000). Additive Logistic Regression: a Statistical View of Boosting, *The Annals of Statistics*, vol. 38(2), pp. 337–374. 15, 17, 59

M. Fritz and B. Schiele (2008). Decomposition, discovery and detection of visual categories using topic models, in *Proceedings of the IEEE Conference on Computer Vision and Pattern Recognition (CVPR) 2008*. 21

A. C. Gallagher and T. Chen (2009). Understanding images of groups of people, in *Proceedings of the IEEE Conference on Computer Vision and Pattern Recognition (CVPR) 2009*. 28

S. Gammeter, A. Ess, T. Jaeggli, K. Schindler, B. Leibe, and L. Van Gool (2008). Articulated Multibody Tracking Under Egomotion, in *Proceedings of the European Conference on Computer Vision (ECCV) 2008*. 39

D. M. Gavrila (2007). A Bayesian, Exemplar-based Approach to Hierarchical Shape Matching, *IEEE Transactions on Pattern Analysis and Machine Intelligence*. 56, 121

D. M. Gavrila and S. Munder (2007). Multi-Cue Pedestrian Detection and Tracking from a Moving Vehicle, *International Journal of Computer Vision*, vol. 73, pp. 41–59. 22, 24, 27, 39, 40, 99, 100, 119

D. M. Gavrila and V. Philomin (1999). Real-time Object Detection for Smart Vehicles, in *Proceedings of the IEEE International Conference on Computer Vision (ICCV) 1999*. 22, 27, 39, 72

D. Geronimo, A. M. Lopez, A. D. Sappa, and T. Graf (2009). Survey on Pedestrian Detection for Advanced Driver Assistance Systems, *IEEE Transactions on Pattern Analysis and Machine Intelligence*, vol. 99(PrePrints). 17

D. Gerónimo, A. Sappa, A. López, and D. Ponsa (2005). Adaptive image sampling and windows classification for on-board pedestrian detection, in *Proceedings of the Proceedings of the International Conference on Computer Vision Systems (ICVS) 2005*. 121

D. Gerónimo, A. Sappa, D. Ponsa, and A. López (2010). 2D-3D based on-board pedestrian detection system, *Computer Vision and Image Understanding*, vol. in press. 39

J. J. Gibson (1979). *The Ecological Approach to Visual Perception*, Houghton Mifflin, Boston, MA. 1, 55

J. Giebel, D. Gavrila, and C. Schnörr (2004). A Bayesian Framework for Multi-cue 3D Object Tracking, in *Proceedings of the European Conference on Computer Vision (ECCV) 2004*. 35

W. Gilks, S. Richardson, and D. Spiegelhalter (Eds.) (1995). *Markov Chain Monte Carlo in Practice*, Chapman & Hall. 103

S. Gould, R. Fulton, and D. Koller (2009a). Decomposing a Scene into Geometric and Semantically Consistent Regions, in *Proceedings of the IEEE International Conference on Computer Vision (ICCV) 2009*. 38, 40

S. Gould, T. Gao, and D. Koller (2009b). Region-based Segmentation and Object Detection, in *Advances in Neural Information Processing Systems (NIPS) 2009*. 32, 38, 40

H. Grabner and H. Bischof (2006). On-line Boosting and Vision, in *Proceedings of the IEEE Conference on Computer Vision and Pattern Recognition (CVPR) 2006*. 34, 120

H. Grabner, C. Leistner, and H. Bischof (2008). Semi-supervised On-Line Boosting for Robust Tracking, in *Proceedings of the European Conference on Computer Vision (ECCV) 2008*. 34, 120

P. J. Green (1995). Reversible jump Markov chain Monte Carlo computation and Bayesian model determination, *Biometrika*, vol. 82(4). 103

T. L. Griffiths and M. Steyvers (2004). Finding scientific topics, *Proceedings of the National Academy of Sciences of the United States of America*, vol. 101(Suppl 1), pp. 5228–5235. 21

G. Grubb, A. Zelinsky, L. Nilsson, and M. Rilbe (2004). 3D vision sensing for improved pedestrian safety, in *Proceedings of the IEEE International Conference on Intelligent Vehicles (IV) 2004*. 38, 40

I. Haritaoglu, D. Harwood, and L. Davis (2000). W4: Real-time Surveillance of People and their Activities, *IEEE Transactions on Pattern Analysis and Machine Intelligence*, vol. 22(8), pp. 809–830. 33

R. I. Hartley and A. Zisserman (2004). *Multiple View Geometry in Computer Vision*, Cambridge University Press, 2nd edn. 9

H. Hattori, A. Seki, M. Nishiyama, and T. Watanabe (2009). Stereo-Based Pedestrian Detection using Multiple Patterns, in *Proceedings of the British Machine Vision Conference (BMVC) 2009*. 23

X. He, R. S. Zemel, and M. Á. Carreira-Perpiñán (2004). Multiscale Conditional Random Fields for Image Labeling, in *Proceedings of the IEEE Conference on Computer Vision and Pattern Recognition (CVPR) 2004*. 30, 86, 93

X. He, R. S. Zemel, and D. Ray (2006). Learning and Incorporating Top-Down Cues in Image Segmentation, in *Proceedings of the European Conference on Computer Vision (ECCV) 2006*. 30

G. Heitz and D. Koller (2008). Learning spatial context: using stuff to find things, in *Proceedings of the European Conference on Computer Vision (ECCV) 2008*. 28

Y. Hel-Or and H. Hel-Or (2005). Real-time pattern matching using projection kernels, *IEEE Transactions on Pattern Analysis and Machine Intelligence*, vol. 27, pp. 1430–1445. 91, 92, 108, 127

A. Hohm, C. Wojek, B. Schiele, and H. Winner (2008). Multi-Level Sensorfusion and Computer-Vision Algorithms within a Driver Assistance System for Avoiding Overtaking-Accidents, in *FISITA 2008 World Automotive Congress 2008*. 123

D. Hoiem, A. A. Efros, and M. Hebert (2006). Putting Objects in Perspective, in *Proceedings of the IEEE Conference on Computer Vision and Pattern Recognition (CVPR) 2006*. 1

D. Hoiem, A. A. Efros, and M. Hebert (2007a). Recovering Surface Layout from an Image, *International Journal of Computer Vision*, vol. 75(1), pp. 151–172. 37, 38

D. Hoiem, A. A. Efros, and M. Hebert (2008a). Closing the Loop on Scene Interpretation, in *Proceedings of the IEEE Conference on Computer Vision and Pattern Recognition (CVPR) 2008*. 38

D. Hoiem, A. A. Efros, and M. Hebert (2008b). Putting Objects in Perspective, *International Journal of Computer Vision*, vol. 80(1), pp. 3–15. 38, 86, 100, 116

D. Hoiem, C. Rother, and J. Winn (2007b). 3D LayoutCRF for Multi-View Object Class Recognition and Segmentation, in *Proceedings of the IEEE Conference on Computer Vision and Pattern Recognition (CVPR) 2007*. 19

C. Huang, B. Wu, and R. Nevatia (2008). Robust object tracking by hierarchical association of detection responses, in *Proceedings of the European Conference on Computer Vision (ECCV) 2008*. 35

S. Ioffe and D. A. Forsyth (2001). Probabilistic Methods for Finding People, *International Journal of Computer Vision*, pp. 45–68. 17

M. Isard and A. Blake (1998). CONDENSATION–Conditional Density Propagation for Visual Tracking, in *International Journal of Computer Vision 1998*. 34

M. Isard and J. MacCormick (2001). BraMBLe: A bayesian multipleblob tracker, in *Proceedings of the IEEE International Conference on Computer Vision (ICCV) 2001*. 33, 103

T. Jaeggli, E. Koller-Meier, and L. Van Gool (2009). Learning Generative Models for Multi-Activity Body Pose Estimation, *International Journal of Computer Vision*, vol. 83(2), pp. 121–134. 40

H. Jiang, S. Fels, and J. J. Little (2007). A linear programming approach for multiple object tracking, in *Proceedings of the IEEE Conference on Computer Vision and Pattern Recognition (CVPR) 2007*. 35

T. Joachims (1999). Making Large–Scale SVM Learning Practical, in B. Schölkopf, C. J. C. Burges, and A. J. Smola (eds.), *Advances in Kernel Methods — Support Vector Learning 1999*, pp. 169–184, MIT Press, Cambridge, MA. 45

T. Kadir and M. Brady (2001). Saliency, Scale and Image Description, *International Journal of Computer Vision*, vol. 45(2), pp. 83–105. 17

R. Kalman (1960). A New Approach to Linear Filtering and Prediction Problems, *Trans. of ASME Journal of Basic Engineering*, pp. 35–45. 34, 39, 89

A. Kapoor and J. Winn (2006). Located Hidden Random Fields: Learning Discriminative Parts for Object Detection, in *Proceedings of the European Conference on Computer Vision (ECCV) 2006*. 19

R. Kaucic, A. G. Perera, G. Brooksby, J. Kaufhold, and A. Hoogs (2005). A Unified Framework for Tracking through Occlusions and Across Sensor Gaps, in *Proceedings of the IEEE Conference on Computer Vision and Pattern Recognition (CVPR) 2005*. 35, 100

Z. Khan, T. Balch, and F. Dellaert (2005). MCMC-Based particle Filtering for Tracking a Variable Number of Interacting Targets, *IEEE Transactions on Pattern Analysis and Machine Intelligence*, vol. 27(11), pp. 1805–1819. 34, 36

T.-K. Kim and R. Cipolla (2008). MCBoost: Multiple Classifier Boosting for Perceptual Co-clustering of Images and Visual Features, in *Advances in Neural Information Processing Systems (NIPS) 2008*. 10, 60

T. Ko, S. Soatto, and D. Estrin (2008). Background Subtraction on Distributions, in *Proceedings of the European Conference on Computer Vision (ECCV) 2008*. 9, 55

P. Kohli, L. Ladicky, and P. H. S. Torr (2009). Robust Higher Order Potentials for Enforcing Label Consistency, *International Journal of Computer Vision*, vol. 82(3), pp. 302–324. 31

S. Krotosky and M. Trivedi (2007). A Comparison of Color and Infrared Stereo Approaches to Pedestrian Detection, in *Proceedings of the IEEE International Conference on Intelligent Vehicles (IV) 2007*. 24

H. Kruppa and B. Schiele (2003). Using Local Context To Improve Face Detection, in *Proceedings of the British Machine Vision Conference (BMVC) 2003*. 29

F. R. Kschischang, B. J. Frey, and H.-A. Loeliger (2001). Factor graphs and the sum-product algorithm, *IEEE Transactions on Information Theory*, vol. 47. 106

S. Kumar and M. Hebert (2003). Discriminative Random Fields: A Discriminative Framework for Contextual Interaction in Classification, in *Proceedings of the IEEE International Conference on Computer Vision (ICCV) 2003*. 29

S. Kumar and M. Hebert (2005). A Hierarchical Field Framework for Unified Context-Based Classification, in *Proceedings of the IEEE International Conference on Computer Vision (ICCV) 2005*. 30, 31, 86, 87, 93

R. Labayrade, D. Aubert, and J.-P. Tarel (2002). Real time obstacle detection on non flat road geometry through 'v-disparity' representation, in *Proceedings of the IEEE International Conference on Intelligent Vehicles (IV) 2002*. 37, 38

L. Ladicky, C. Russell, P. Kohli, and P. Torr (2009). Associative hierarchical CRFs for object class image segmentation, in *Proceedings of the IEEE International Conference on Computer Vision (ICCV) 2009*. 31, 32

J. D. Lafferty, A. McCallum, and F. C. N. Pereira (2001). Conditional random fields: probabilistic models for segmenting and labeling sequence data, in *Proceedings of International Conference on Machine learning 2001*. 28

C. H. Lampert and M. B. Blaschko (2008). A Multiple Kernel Learning Approach to Joint Multi-class Object Detection, in *Pattern Recognition, Proceedings of the DAGM Symposium 2008*. 28

C. H. Lampert, M. B. Blaschko, and T. Hofmann (2009). Efficient Subwindow Search: A Branch and Bound Framework for Object Localization, *IEEE Transactions on Pattern Analysis and Machine Intelligence*, vol. 31, pp. 2129–2142. 46

O. Lanz (2006). Approximate Bayesian Multibody Tracking, *IEEE Transactions on Pattern Analysis and Machine Intelligence*, vol. 28(9), pp. 1436–1449. 35

I. Laptev (2006). Improvements of Object Detection Using Boosted Histograms, in *Proceedings of the British Machine Vision Conference (BMVC) 2006*. 21, 72

D. Larlus, J. Verbeek, and F. Jurie (2010). Category Level Object Segmentation by Combining Bag-of-Words Models with Dirichlet Processes and Random Fields, *International Journal of Computer Vision*, vol. 88(2), pp. 238–253. 31, 86

B. Leibe, A. Leonardis, and B. Schiele (2008a). Robust Object Detection with Interleaved Categorization and Segmentation, *International Journal of Computer Vision*, vol. 77(1-3), pp. 259–289. 18, 34, 39, 41, 46

B. Leibe, K. Schindler, N. Cornelis, and L. Van Gool (2008b). Coupled Detection and Tracking from Static Cameras and Moving Vehicles, *IEEE Transactions on Pattern Analysis and Machine Intelligence*, vol. 30(10), pp. 1683–1698. 35, 39

B. Leibe, E. Seemann, and B. Schiele (2005). Pedestrian Detection in Crowded Scenes, in *Proceedings of the IEEE Conference on Computer Vision and Pattern Recognition (CVPR) 2005*. 18, 45

K. Levi and Y. Weiss (2004). Learning Object Detection from a Small Number of Examples: The Importance of Good Features, in *Proceedings of the IEEE Conference on Computer Vision and Pattern Recognition (CVPR) 2004*. 51

Y. Li, C. Huang, and R. Nevatia (2009). Learning to Associate: HybridBoosted Multi-Target Tracker for Crowded Scene, in *Proceedings of the IEEE Conference on Computer Vision and Pattern Recognition (CVPR) 2009*. 36

Z. Lin and L. S. Davis (2008). A Pose-Invariant Descriptor for Human Detection and Segmentation, in *Proceedings of the European Conference on Computer Vision (ECCV) 2008*. 22, 56

Z. Lin, G. Hua, and L. S. Davis (2009). Multiple instance feature for robust part-based object detection, in *Proceedings of the IEEE Conference on Computer Vision and Pattern Recognition (CVPR) 2009*. 25

Y. Liu, S. Shan, W. Zhang, X. Chen, and W. Gao (2009). Granularity-tunable gradients partition (GGP) descriptors for human detection, in *Proceedings of the IEEE Conference on Computer Vision and Pattern Recognition (CVPR) 2009*. 22

D. G. Lowe (2004). Distinctive Image Features from Scale-Invariant Keypoints, *International Journal of Computer Vision*, vol. 60(2), pp. 91–110. 19, 21

M. Mählisch, M. Oberlander, O. Lohlein, D. Gavrila, and W. Ritter (2005). A Multiple Detector Approach to Low-Resolution FIR Pedestrian Recognition, in *Proceedings of the IEEE International Conference on Intelligent Vehicles (IV) 2005*. 24

S. Maji, A. Berg, and J. Malik (2008). Classification using intersection kernel SVMs is efficient, in *Proceedings of the IEEE Conference on Computer Vision and Pattern Recognition (CVPR) 2008*. 21, 47, 56, 59

S. Maji and J. Malik (2009). Object detection using a max-margin Hough transform, in *Proceedings of the IEEE Conference on Computer Vision and Pattern Recognition (CVPR) 2009*. 19

J. C. McCall and M. M. Trivedi (2006). Video-based lane estimation and tracking for driver assistance: survey, system, and evaluation, *IEEE Transactions on Intelligent Transportation Systems*, vol. 7(1), pp. 20–37. 38

A. McCallum, K. Rohanimanesh, and C. Sutton (2003). Dynamic Conditional Random Fields for Jointly Labeling Multiple Sequences, in *NIPS Workshop on Syntax, Semantics 2003*. 32, 85, 86

K. Mikolajczyk, B. Leibe, and B. Schiele (2006). Multiple Object Class Detection with a Generative Model, in *Proceedings of the IEEE Conference on Computer Vision and Pattern Recognition (CVPR) 2006*. 18

K. Mikolajczyk and C. Schmid (2005). A Performance Evaluation of Local Descriptors, *IEEE Transactions on Pattern Analysis and Machine Intelligence*, vol. 27(10), pp. 1615–1630. 45

K. Mikolajczyk, C. Schmid, and A. Zisserman (2004). Human detection based on a probabilistic assembly of robust part detectors, in *Proceedings of the European Conference on Computer Vision (ECCV) 2004*. 18, 42

A. Mittal and L. Davis (2003). M2Tracker: a multi-view approach to segmenting and tracking people in a cluttered scene, *International Journal of Computer Vision*, vol. 51, pp. 189–203. 33

A. Mohan, C. Papageorgiou, and T. Poggio (2001). Example-Based Object Detection in Images by Components, *IEEE Transactions on Pattern Analysis and Machine Intelligence*, vol. 23(4), pp. 349–361. 25

S. Munder and D. M. Gavrila (2006). An Experimental Study on Pedestrian Classification, *IEEE Transactions on Pattern Analysis and Machine Intelligence*, vol. 28(11), pp. 1863–1868. 22, 26, 42, 49, 51, 72, 73

K. Murphy, A. Torralba, and W. T. Freeman (2003). Using the Forest to See the Trees: A Graphical Model Relating Features, Objects, and Scenes, in *Advances in Neural Information Processing Systems (NIPS) 2003*. 28

S. Nedevschi, R. Danescu, D. Frentiu, T. Graf, and R. Schmidt (2004). High accuracy stereovision approach for obstacle detection on non-planar roads, in *Proceedings of IEEE Intelligent Engineering Systems 2004*. 37

S. Nedevschi, R. Danescu, T. Marita, F. Oniga, C. Pocol, S. Sobol, C. Tomiuc, C. Vancea, M. M. Meinecke, T. Graf, T. B. To, and M. A. Obojski (2007). A Sensor for Urban Driving Assistance Systems Based on Dense Stereovision, in *Proceedings of the IEEE International Conference on Intelligent Vehicles (IV) 2007*. 37

P. Nillius, J. Sullivan, and S. Carlsson (2006). Multi-Target Tracking-Linking Identities Using Bayesian Network Inference, in *Proceedings of the IEEE Conference on Computer Vision and Pattern Recognition (CVPR) 2006*. 36

E. Nowak, F. Jurie, and B. Triggs (2006). Sampling Strategies for Bag-of-Features Image Classification, in *Proceedings of the European Conference on Computer Vision (ECCV) 2006*. 72

K. Nummiaro, E. Koller-Meier, and L. Van Gool (2003). An adaptive color-based particle filter, *Image and Vision Computing*, vol. 21(1), pp. 99–110. 35

T. Ojala, M. Pietikainen, and T. Maenpaa (2002). Multiresolution Gray-Scale and Rotation Invariant Texture Classification with Local Binary Patterns, *IEEE Transactions on Pattern Analysis and Machine Intelligence*, vol. 24(7), pp. 971–987. 25, 29

K. Okuma, A. Taleghani, N. de Freitas, J. Little, and D. Lowe (2004). A Boosted Particle Filter: Multitarget Detection and Tracking, in *Proceedings of the European Conference on Computer Vision (ECCV) 2004*. 33, 36, 100

P. Ott and M. Everingham (2009). Implicit Color Segmentation Features for Pedestrian and Object Detection, in *Proceedings of the IEEE International Conference on Computer Vision (ICCV) 2009*. 25

N. C. Oza (2001). *Online Ensemble Learning*, Ph.D. thesis, The University of California, Berkeley, CA. 34

C. Papageorgiou and T. Poggio (2000). A Trainable System for Object Detection, *International Journal of Computer Vision*, vol. 38(1), pp. 15–33. 20, 25, 39, 42, 43, 44, 47, 48, 49, 50, 58, 72, 125

S. Pellegrini, A. Ess, K. Schindler, and L. Van Gool (2009). You'll Never Walk Alone: Modeling Social Behavior for Multi-target Tracking, in *Proceedings of the IEEE International Conference on Computer Vision (ICCV) 2009*. 122

A. G. A. Perera, C. Srinivas, A. Hoogs, G. Brooksby, and W. Hu (2006). Multi-object tracking through simultaneous long occlusions and split-merge conditions, in *Proceedings of the IEEE Conference on Computer Vision and Pattern Recognition (CVPR) 2006*. 35

J. Platt (2000). Probabilistic outputs for support vector machines and comparison to regularized likelihood methods, in *Advances in Large Margin Classifiers 2000*. 88

F. M. Porikli (2005). Integral Histogram: A Fast Way To Extract Histograms in Cartesian Spaces, in *Proceedings of the IEEE Conference on Computer Vision and Pattern Recognition (CVPR) 2005*. 26

V. Prisacariu and I. Reid (2009). fastHOG - a real-time GPU implementation of HOG, Technical report 2310/09, Department of Engineering Science, Oxford University. 27

A. Quattoni, S. Wang, L.-P. Morency, M. Collins, and T. Darrell (2007). Hidden Conditional Random Fields, *IEEE Transactions on Pattern Analysis and Machine Intelligence*, vol. 29, pp. 1848–1852. 19

A. Rabinovich, A. Vedaldi, C. Galleguillos, E. Wiewiora, and S. Belongie (2007). Objects in Context, in *Proceedings of the IEEE International Conference on Computer Vision (ICCV) 2007*. 30

M. Rapus, S. Munder, G. Baratoff, and J. Denzler (2008). Pedestrian Recognition Using Combined Low-Resolution Depth and Intensity Images, in *Proceedings of the IEEE International Conference on Intelligent Vehicles (IV) 2008*. 23

C. Rasmussen and G. Hager (2001). Probabilistic Data Association Methods for Tracking Complex Visual Objects, *IEEE Transactions on Pattern Analysis and Machine Intelligence*, vol. 23(6), pp. 560–576. 33

D. Reid (1979). An Algorithm for Tracking Multiple Targets, *IEEE Transactions on Automatic Control*, vol. 24(6), pp. 843–854. 33

M. Rohrbach, M. Enzweiler, and D. M. Gavrila (2009). High-Level Fusion of Depth and Intensity for Pedestrian Classification, in *Pattern Recognition, Proceedings of the DAGM Symposium 2009*. 22

B. Russell, A. Torralba, K. P. Murphy, and W. T. Freeman (2008). LabelMe: A Database and Web-Based Tool for Image Annotation, *International Journal of Computer Vision*, vol. 77(1-3), pp. 157–173. 93

P. Sabzmeydani and G. Mori (2007). Detecting Pedestrians by Learning Shapelet Features, in *Proceedings of the IEEE Conference on Computer Vision and Pattern Recognition (CVPR) 2007*. 22, 43, 44, 47, 56

A. Saxena, S. H. Chung, and A. Y. Ng (2008). 3-D Depth Reconstruction from a Single Still Image, *International Journal of Computer Vision*, vol. 76(1), pp. 53–69. 37

B. Schiele, M. Andriluka, N. Majer, S. Roth, and C. Wojek (2009). Visual People Detection: Different Models, Comparison and Discussion, in *Proceedings of the IEEE ICRA 2009 Workshop on People Detection and Tracking 2009*. 12

B. Schiele and C. Wojek (2009). *Kamerabasierte Fussgängerdetektion*, chapter Kamerabasierte Fussgängerdetektion, Vieweg+Teubner Verlag. 12

H. Schneiderman and T. Kanade (2004). Object Detection Using the Statistics of Parts, *International Journal of Computer Vision*, vol. 56(3), pp. 151–177. 20, 29

P. Schnitzspan, M. Fritz, S. Roth, and B. Schiele (2009). Discriminative Structure Learning of Hierarchical Representations for Object Detection, in *Proceedings of the IEEE Conference on Computer Vision and Pattern Recognition (CVPR) 2009*. 19

P. Schnitzspan, M. Fritz, and B. Schiele (2008). Hierarchical Support Vector Random Fields: Joint Training to Combine Local and Global Features, in *Proceedings of the European Conference on Computer Vision (ECCV) 2008*. 19

P. Schnitzspan, S. Roth, and B. Schiele (2010). Automatic Discovery of Meaningful Object Parts with Latent CRFs, in *Proceedings of the IEEE Conference on Computer Vision and Pattern Recognition (CVPR) 2010*. 19

B. Schoelkopf and A. J. Smola (2001). *Learning with Kernels: Support Vector Machines, Regularization, Optimization, and Beyond*, MIT Press. 15

F. Schroff, A. Criminisi, and A. Zisserman (2008). Object Class Segmentation using Random Forests, in *Proceedings of the British Machine Vision Conference (BMVC) 2008*. 30

W. Schwartz, A. Kembhavi, D. Harwood, and L. Davis (2009). Human Detection using Partial Least Squares Analysis, in *Proceedings of the IEEE International Conference on Computer Vision (ICCV) 2009*. 24

E. Seemann, B. Leibe, K. Mikolajczyk, and B. Schiele (2005). An Evaluation of Local Shape-Based Features for Pedestrian Detection, in *Proceedings of the British Machine Vision Conference (BMVC) 2005*. 18, 42, 43

E. Seemann, B. Leibe, and B. Schiele (2006). Multi-Aspect Detection of Articulated Objects, in *Proceedings of the IEEE Conference on Computer Vision and Pattern Recognition (CVPR) 2006*. 18, 42, 45, 56

E. Seemann and B. Schiele (2006). Cross-Articulation Learning for Robust Detection of Pedestrians, in *Pattern Recognition, Proceedings of the DAGM Symposium 2006*. 18

V. Sharma and J. Davis (2007). Integrating Appearance and Motion Cues for Simultaneous Detection and Segmentation of Pedestrians, in *Proceedings of the IEEE International Conference on Computer Vision (ICCV) 2007*. 9, 55

A. Shashua, Y. Gdalyahu, and G. Hayun (2004). Pedestrian detection for driving assistance systems: Single-frame classification and system level performance, in *Proceedings of the IEEE International Conference on Intelligent Vehicles (IV) 2004*. 20, 22, 27, 56, 72

J. Shi and J. Malik (2000). Normalized Cuts and Image Segmentation, *IEEE Transactions on Pattern Analysis and Machine Intelligence*, vol. 22(8), pp. 888–905. 28, 29

J. Shotton, M. Johnson, and R. Cipolla (2008). Semantic texton forests for image categorization and segmentation, in *Proceedings of the IEEE Conference on Computer Vision and Pattern Recognition (CVPR) 2008*. 30

J. Shotton, J. Winn, C. Rother, and A. Criminisi (2006). *TextonBoost*: Joint Appearance, Shape and Context Modeling for Multi-Class Object Recognition and Segmentation, in *Proceedings of the European Conference on Computer Vision (ECCV) 2006*. 86, 93

J. Shotton, J. Winn, C. Rother, and A. Criminisi (2009). TextonBoost for Image Understanding: Multi-Class Object Recognition and Segmentation by Jointly Modeling Texture, Layout, and Context, *International Journal of Computer Vision*, vol. 81(1), pp. 2–23. 29, 32

M. Soga, T. Kato, M. Ohta, and Y. Ninomiya (2005). Pedestrian Detection with Stereo Vision, in *IEEE International Conference on Data Engineering 2005*. 20

X. Song and R. Nevatia (2007). Detection and Tracking of Moving Vehicles in Crowded Scenes, in *Proceedings of the IEEE Workshop on Motion and Video Computing (WMVC) 2007*. 35

M. Stark, M. Goesele, and B. Schiele (2009). A Shape-Based Object Class Model for Knowledge Transfer, in *Proceedings of the IEEE International Conference on Computer Vision (ICCV) 2009*. 18, 46

C. Stauffer and W. E. L. Grimson (2000). Learning Patterns of Activity Using Real-Time Tracking, *IEEE Transactions on Pattern Analysis and Machine Intelligence*, vol. 22(8), pp. 747–757. 9, 55

P. Sturgess, K. Alahari, L. Ladicky, and P. Torr (2009). Combining Appearance and Structure from Motion Features for Road Scene Understanding, in *Proceedings of the British Machine Vision Conference (BMVC) 2009*. 32

F. Suard, A. Rakotomamonjy, A. Bensrhair, and A. Broggi (2006). Pedestrian Detection using Infrared images and Histograms of Oriented Gradients, in *Proceedings of the IEEE International Conference on Intelligent Vehicles (IV) 2006*. 24

E. B. Sudderth, A. Torralba, W. T. Freeman, and A. S. Willsky (2008). Describing Visual Scenes Using Transformed Objects and Parts, *International Journal of Computer Vision*, vol. 77(1-3), pp. 291–330. 31

Z. Sun, G. Bebis, and R. Miller (2006). On-Road Vehicle Detection: A Review, *IEEE Transactions on Pattern Analysis and Machine Intelligence*, vol. 28, pp. 694–711. 17

C. Sutton and A. McCallum (2005). Piecewise Training for Undirected Models, in *21th Annual Conference on Uncertainty in Artificial Intelligence (UAI-05) 2005*. 90, 91

B. Taskar, V. Chatalbashev, D. Koller, and C. Guestrin (2005). Learning structured prediction models: a large margin approach, in *Proceedings of International Conference on Machine learning 2005*. 25

A. Torralba (2003). Contextual Priming for Object Detection, *International Journal of Computer Vision*, vol. 53(2), pp. 169–191. 1, 2, 28, 86

A. Torralba, K. P. Murphy, and W. T. Freeman (2005). Contextual Models for Object Detection Using Boosted Random Fields, in *Advances in Neural Information Processing Systems (NIPS) 2005*. 30, 86

A. Torralba, K. P. Murphy, and W. T. Freeman (2007). Sharing Visual Features for Multiclass and Multiview Object Detection, *IEEE Transactions on Pattern Analysis and Machine Intelligence*, vol. 29(5), pp. 854–869. 87, 107, 121

D. Tran and D. Forsyth (2008). Configuration Estimates Improve Pedestrian Finding, in *Advances in Neural Information Processing Systems (NIPS) 2008*. 25

J. Tsotsos (1987). Image understanding, *The Encyclopedia of Artificial Intelligence*. 15

Z. Tu, X. Chen, A. Yuille, and S. Zhu (2005). Image Parsing: Unifying Segmentation, Detection, and Recognition, *International Journal of Computer Vision*, vol. 63(2). 28

M. Turtinen and M. Pietikäinen (2006). Contextual analysis of textured scene images, in *Proceedings of the British Machine Vision Conference (BMVC) 2006*. 29

T. Tuytelaars and C. Schmid (2007). Vector Quantizing Feature Space with a Regular Lattice, in *Proceedings of the IEEE International Conference on Computer Vision (ICCV) 2007*. 72

O. Tuzel, F. Porikli, and P. Meer (2007). Human Detection via Classification on Riemannian Manifolds, in *Proceedings of the IEEE Conference on Computer Vision and Pattern Recognition (CVPR) 2007*. 72

O. Tuzel, F. Porikli, and P. Meer (2008). Pedestrian Detection via Classification on Riemannian Manifolds, *IEEE Transactions on Pattern Analysis and Machine Intelligence*, vol. 30(10), pp. 1713–1727. 21

M. Varma and D. Ray (2007). Learning the Discriminative Power-Invariance Trade-Off, in *Proceedings of the IEEE International Conference on Computer Vision (ICCV) 2007*. 56, 66

M. Varma and A. Zisserman (2002). Classifying Images of Materials: Achieving Viewpoint and Illumination Indepence, in *Proceedings of the European Conference on Computer Vision (ECCV) 2002*. 92, 94, 108

A. Vedaldi, V. Gulshan, M. Varma, and A. Zisserman (2009). Multiple Kernels for Object Detection, in *Proceedings of the IEEE International Conference on Computer Vision (ICCV) 2009*. 24

J. Verbeek and B. Triggs (2007). Region Classification with Markov Field Aspect Models, in *Proceedings of the IEEE Conference on Computer Vision and Pattern Recognition (CVPR) 2007*. 30

P. A. Viola and M. J. Jones (2004). Robust Real-Time Face Detection, *International Journal of Computer Vision*, vol. 57(2), pp. 137–154. 20, 23, 24, 26, 33, 42, 43, 47, 51, 56, 60, 72

P. A. Viola, M. J. Jones, and D. Snow (2005). Detecting pedestrians using patterns of motion and appearance, *International Journal of Computer Vision*, vol. 63(2), pp. 153–161. 23, 27, 55

S. V. N. Vishwanathan, N. N. Schraudolph, M. W. Schmidt, and K. P. Murphy (2006). Accelerated training of conditional random fields with stochastic gradient methods, in *Proceedings of International Conference on Machine learning 2006*. 91

J. Vogel and B. Schiele (2007). Semantic Modeling of Natural Scenes for Content-Based Image Retrieval, *International Journal of Computer Vision*, vol. 72(2), pp. 133–157. 29

S. Walk, N. Majer, K. Schindler, and B. Schiele (2010). New features and insights for pedestrian detection, in *Proceedings of the IEEE Conference on Computer Vision and Pattern Recognition (CVPR) 2010*. 25

C. C. Wang, C. Thorpe, S. Thrun, M. Hebert, and H. Durrant-Whyte (2007). Simultaneous localization, mapping and moving object tracking, *The International Journal of Robotics Research*, vol. 26, pp. 889–916. 3

X. Wang, T. X. Han, and S. Yan (2009). An HOG-LBP Human Detector with Partial Occlusion Handling, in *Proceedings of the IEEE International Conference on Computer Vision (ICCV) 2009*. 25

Y. Wang and Q. Ji (2005). A Dynamic Conditional Random Field Model for Object Segmentation in Image Sequences, in *Proceedings of the IEEE Conference on Computer Vision and Pattern Recognition (CVPR) 2005*. 32

M. Weber, M. Welling, and P. Perona (2000). Unsupervised Learning of Models for Recognition, in *Proceedings of the European Conference on Computer Vision (ECCV) 2000*. 17

A. Wedel, C. Rabe, H. Badino, H. Loose, U. Franke, and D. Cremers (2009). B-Spline Modeling of Road Surfaces with an Application to Free Space Estimation, *IEEE Transactions on Intelligent Transportation Systems*, vol. 10(4), pp. 572–583. 122

J. Winn and J. Shotton (2006). The Layout Consistent Random Field for Recognizing and Segmenting Partially Occluded Objects, in *Proceedings of the IEEE Conference on Computer Vision and Pattern Recognition (CVPR) 2006*. 19, 32, 88

C. Wöhler and J. K. Anlauf (1999). An adaptable time-delay neural-network algorithm for image sequence analysis, *IEEE Transactions on Neural Networks*, vol. 10(6), pp. 1531–1536. 23, 26

C. Wojek, G. Dorkó, A. Schulz, and B. Schiele (2008). Sliding-Windows for Rapid Object Class Localization: A Parallel Technique, in *Pattern Recognition, Proceedings of the DAGM Symposium 2008*. 12

C. Wojek, S. Roth, K. Schindler, and B. Schiele (2010). Monocular 3D Scene Modeling and Inference: Understanding Multi-Object Traffic Scenes, in *Proceedings of the European Conference on Computer Vision (ECCV) 2010*. 13

C. Wojek and B. Schiele (2008a). A Dynamic CRF Model for Joint Labeling of Object and Scene Classes, in *Proceedings of the European Conference on Computer Vision (ECCV) 2008*. 13, 79

C. Wojek and B. Schiele (2008b). A Performance Evaluation of Single and Multi-feature People Detection, in *Pattern Recognition, Proceedings of the DAGM Symposium 2008*. 11, 56

C. Wojek, S. Walk, and B. Schiele (2009). Multi-Cue Onboard Pedestrian Detection, in *Proceedings of the IEEE Conference on Computer Vision and Pattern Recognition (CVPR) 2009*. 12

C. Wren, A. Azarbayejani, T. Darrell, and A. Pentland (1997). Pfinder: Real-Time Tracking of the Human Body, *IEEE Transactions on Pattern Analysis and Machine Intelligence*, vol. 19(7), pp. 780–785. 33

B. Wu and R. Nevatia (2005). Detection of Multiple, Partially Occluded Humans in a Single Image by Bayesian Combination of Edgelet Part Detectors, in *Proceedings of the IEEE International Conference on Computer Vision (ICCV) 2005*. 22, 33, 42

B. Wu and R. Nevatia (2007a). Cluster Boosted Tree Classifier for Multi-View, Multi-Pose Object Detection, in *Proceedings of the IEEE International Conference on Computer Vision (ICCV) 2007*. 22, 56

B. Wu and R. Nevatia (2007b). Detection and Tracking of Multiple, Partially Occluded Humans by Bayesian Combination of Edgelet Part Detectors, *International Journal of Computer Vision*, vol. 75(2), pp. 247–266. 33

B. Wu and R. Nevatia (2008). Optimizing discrimination-efficiency tradeoff in integrating heterogeneous local features for object detection, in *Proceedings of the IEEE Conference on Computer Vision and Pattern Recognition (CVPR) 2008*. 24, 56

J. Xing, H. Ai, and S. Lao (2009). Multi-object tracking through occlusions by local tracklets filtering and global tracklets association with detection responses, in *Proceedings of the IEEE Conference on Computer Vision and Pattern Recognition (CVPR) 2009*. 36

F. Xu, X. Liu, and K. Fujimura (2005). Pedestrian detection and tracking with night vision, *IEEE Transactions on Intelligent Transportation Systems*, vol. 6(1), pp. 63–71. 24

F. Yan, A. Kostin, W. J. Christmas, and J. Kittler (2006). A Novel Data Association Algorithm for Object Tracking in Clutter with Application to Tennis Video Analysis, in *Proceedings of the IEEE Conference on Computer Vision and Pattern Recognition (CVPR) 2006*. 36

Z. Yin and R. Collins (2007). Belief Propagation in a 3D Spatio-temporal MRF for Moving Object Detection, in *Proceedings of the IEEE Conference on Computer Vision and Pattern Recognition (CVPR) 2007*. 32

Q. Yu and G. Medioni (2009). Multiple-Target Tracking by Spatiotemporal Monte Carlo Markov Chain Data Association, *IEEE Transactions on Pattern Analysis and Machine Intelligence*, vol. 31(12), pp. 2196–2210. 35

C. Zach, T. Pock, and H. Bischof (2007). A Duality Based Approach for Realtime $TV - L^1$ Optical Flow, in *Pattern Recognition, Proceedings of the DAGM Symposium 2007*. 57, 58, 59, 65, 69

P. Zehnder, E. Koller-Meier, and L. Van Gool (2008). An Efficient Shared Multi-Class Detection Cascade, in *Proceedings of the British Machine Vision Conference (BMVC) 2008*. 121

L. Zhang, Y. Li, and R. Nevatia (2008). Global Data Association for Multi-Object Tracking Using Network Flows, in *Proceedings of the IEEE Conference on Computer Vision and Pattern Recognition (CVPR) 2008*. 35, 66

L. Zhang and R. Nevatia (2008). Efficient scan-window based object detection using GPGPU, in *Visual Computer Vision on GPU's (CVGPU) 2008*. 27

W. Zhang, G. J. Zelinsky, and D. Samaras (2007). Real-time Accurate Object Detection using Multiple Resolutions, in *Proceedings of the IEEE International Conference on Computer Vision (ICCV) 2007*. 26, 27, 71

L. Zhao and C. Thorpe (2000). Stereo- and neural network-based pedestrian detection, *IEEE Transactions on Intelligent Transportation Systems*, vol. 1(3), pp. 148–154. 20, 21

T. Zhao, R. Nevatia, and B. Wu (2008). Segmentation and Tracking of Multiple Humans in Crowded Environments, *IEEE Transactions on Pattern Analysis and Machine Intelligence*, vol. 30(7), pp. 1198–1211. 34, 36

L. Zhu, Y. Chen, Y. Lin, C. Lin, and A. Yuille (2009). Recursive Segmentation and Recognition Templates for 2D Parsing, in *Advances in Neural Information Processing Systems (NIPS) 2009*. 31

Q. Zhu, S. Avidan, M. Yeh, and K. Cheng (2006). Fast Human Detection Using a Cascade of Histograms of Oriented Gradients, in *Proceedings of the IEEE Conference on Computer Vision and Pattern Recognition (CVPR) 2006*. 26, 27, 71

I want morebooks!

Buy your books fast and straightforward online - at one of world's fastest growing online book stores! Environmentally sound due to Print-on-Demand technologies.

Buy your books online at
www.morebooks.shop

Kaufen Sie Ihre Bücher schnell und unkompliziert online – auf einer der am schnellsten wachsenden Buchhandelsplattformen weltweit! Dank Print-On-Demand umwelt- und ressourcenschonend produziert.

Bücher schneller online kaufen
www.morebooks.shop

KS OmniScriptum Publishing
Brivibas gatve 197
LV-1039 Riga, Latvia
Telefax +371 686 204 55

info@omniscriptum.com
www.omniscriptum.com

Printed by Books on Demand GmbH, Norderstedt / Germany